WOMEN'S HISTORY
FOR BEGINNERS

WOMEN'S HISTORY

FOR BEGINNERS

BONNIE J. MORRIS, Ph.D.
Illustrations by PHILL EVANS

FOR BEGINNERS®

an imprint of Steerforth Press
Hanover, New Hampshire

For Beginners LLC
155 Main Street, Suite 211
Danbury, CT 06810 USA
www.forbeginnersbooks.com

A For Beginners® Documentary Comic Book
Copyright © 2012

Cataloging-in-Publication information is available from the Library of
Congress.

ISBN # 978-1-934389-60-7 Trade

Manufactured in the United States of America

For Beginners® and Beginners Documentary Comic Books® are
published by For Beginners LLC.

First Edition

10 9 8 7 6 5 4 3 2 1

contents

For Roger's pride and joy, the next generation of learners:
Cassidy, Caitlin, Lucas, Greyson, and Sophie

A Women's History Final Exam

Welcome to the history of more than half the world: the history you never learned.

Read through a basic history book—say, a state-approved U.S. history textbook intended for middle-school classrooms—and you're left with the impression that all of human history was achieved by one sex: Male.

Of course, women as well as men lived, worked, reproduced, and died in every era of time. Mothers, daughters, and wives were present at every world event—though seldom as equal participants. But we learn very little about them. Their roles seem to have gone unrecorded. Why?

The simplest answer is the system called *patriarchy*. For most of the past—in Western as well as non-Western history—women were neither free and equal under the law nor believed to be capable of acting independently. Females were subject to control by their fathers, husbands, and other male leaders or owners, through laws, local customs, and religious faiths dictated and adjudicated by men. These systems guaranteed that women remained in the *private sphere*, restricted to domestic roles under the watchful eye of male

1

relatives, although most women worked as hard as men at repetitive daily chores in and around the home. Without property rights, independent income, education, or legally recognized personhood, only the most exceptional women were able to transcend such barriers to become rulers, warriors, scholars, and artists in the *public sphere*. Because so many women were denied access to schooling, it was almost impossible for them to write down their own versions of what really happened during the medieval witch trials, or below stairs in the servants' quarters, or in the slave cabins of Mississippi.

Furthermore, most women were held back from public participation and achievement because they were married very young, typically at puberty, and bound to early pregnancy and the rule of their husband thereafter. Women's actions reflected on the men entrusted with guarding their chastity: Some of the earliest written laws command "good" women to cover their hair, a theme later reinforced in Judaism, Christianity, and Islam, sometimes with a spiritual basis but more often interpreted as preventing anyone other than a husband from looking at a mature female. It might be a source of shame and dishonor to a husband if his wife attracted attention, good or bad, for attention equals looking. As early as 430 B.C., Pericles told other Athenians that women were "not to be talked about for good or for evil among men."[1]

A man might be embarrassed and insulted if his wife made a name for herself separate from his own. Note that we still retain the tradition of a woman taking her husband's name upon marriage; her actions will then be inextricably linked with his own reputation, and except as a question on bureaucratic forms, she will no longer supply her former *maiden name*. She is no longer a maiden. (Who recalls the *maiden name* of Abigail Adams? Eleanor Roosevelt? Betty Ford?) The most recognized women in America—First Ladies— are of course known by their married names. At most, a few choose to bury their original family name in the middle, when they continue using it at all: e.g., Hillary Rodham Clinton. Name changes at marriage also mask or alter

---

[1] Thucydides on Pericles, cited in Helga Harriman, *Women in the Western Heritage*. Dushkin Publishing, 1995; p. 64.

the woman's original ethnicity: My own mother lost her Jewish family name (Schiller) at marriage, and accepted my father's Welsh and Protestant surname (Morris). My childhood schoolmate, Sangita Bhasin, who emigrated from India as a child and grew up to become a doctor in America, married a Jewish man. Today her patients know her as Dr. Rosengarten.

When women of the past were denied access to the roles and activities available to their brothers and sons, they funneled their own creative talent and human spirit into sheer survival. Much of that legacy may be seen in the material culture women invented for domestic life: tools, quilts, birthing stools, textiles, and cooking utensils. Because objects meant for daily use and survival in the home sphere lacked the prestige of "real" art, women's history courses, too, are sometimes laughed at as "basket weaving"— an insult which reveals much more than intended. Women's work itself has been judged as both natural and personal, repetitive and trivial, unfit for history books; whereas men's roles in the public sphere were celebrated as worthy: events and breakthroughs of politics, commerce, and culture.[2] But in examining the past with a lens wide enough to encompass both sexes, historians are now beginning to recover a more complete record of human life and human achievement.

Where women and men have played different roles, those very differences tell us a great deal about power, citizenship, and democratic ideals. We may acknowledge that our foremothers held different but equally important functions in human history. Still, most of what is described in *history* is, indeed, "his story," the lives and writings of *great men*.

---

[2] A good source discussing this division of work in Colonial America is Mary Beth Norton's *Liberty's Daughters*.

Pop quiz: How much actual women's history do you know? In terms of your own family, you're probably well acquainted with the life stories of your mother, grandmothers and aunts. We're certainly taught to *honor* our mothers, for female caregivers shape our lives, serving as our earliest role models. You may have been raised by the combined efforts of a single mom, female babysitters, and day-care workers, female elementary-school teachers, school and camp counselors, social workers, coaches, and tutors. You've probably worked for more than one female employer by now; had several consultations with a female doctor; you may have female friends or relatives presently serving in the military; you may have voted for a female candidate in a local or national election. Taking all of this into account, you may feel well-satisfied that today's women have the same opportunities as men, and it's not hard to find statistics showing how far we've come. Female students now outnumber males on most American college campuses.

Despite the visibility and power of women in today's society, most of us remain sadly uninformed about the struggles of our foremothers. Thinking back, how much did you learn about women's contributions to history when you were in school? Were women even represented in the history books assigned to you? How many "famous women" can you name who lived before the twentieth century? Before 1960? Can you name three women inventors?

Here are fifty final-exam questions from some of my women's history courses at George Washington University and Georgetown. See how many answers you know.

1. What is the Venus of Willendorf?

2. Who are Nefertiti and Hatshepsut?

3. Who was Sappho, and where did she live?

4. Which Greek goddess is said to have been born from the head of her father?

5. What happened to Hypatia?

6. What did the sixth-century Salic Law prevent women from inheriting?

7. Who was Hildegard of Bingen?

8. Who led men in the battle to save France, only to be burned at the stake for heresy?

9. Which queen ordered the expulsion of Jews and Muslims from Spain?

10. Which female pirate famously conducted sea raids from her Irish hideout in the sixteenth century?

11. What is the *Malleus Maleficiarum*?

12. In what year were the first African women brought to Colonial America as slaves?

13. Who was the slave who bore Thomas Jefferson's children?

14. Who warned her powerful husband that he'd better "remember the ladies"?

15. Name the young woman who fought in the American Revolution disguised as a boy named Robert Shurtleff.

16. Who was Phillis Wheatley?

17. Who was the Hottentot Venus?

18. When was the first women's rights convention held in Seneca Falls, New York?

19. Who was the first woman admitted to medical school in the United States?

20. Who founded the Red Cross?

21. Who founded Bryn Mawr College?

22   What is Amelia Bloomer best known for?

23. Can you name three female inventors?

24. What were the Comstock Laws?

25. When was the Triangle Factory fire?

26. Who was the first female member of Congress?

27. In what year did Margaret Sanger open the first birth-control clinic in the United States?

28. In what year did American women win the vote? Can you name the amendment?

29. Who led the Russian women's "Battalion of Death" in World War I?

30. When were women first allowed to participate in the Olympic Games?

31. What was the name of Radclyffe Hall's scandalous 1928 novel?

32. Who was the first woman to win a Nobel Peace Prize?

33. Who founded the Women's Army Corps?

34. Who was Hannah Senesh?

35. Name two players from the All-American Girls' baseball league.

36. Who was the first black woman to win an Olympic gold medal?

37. When did Simone de Beauvoir publish *The Second Sex*?

38. What is *Griswold v. Connecticut*?

39. When were women first admitted to Yale University?

40. Which black woman ran for President of the United States in 1972?

41. When were women first admitted to West Point and the Naval Academy?

42. When were women of any nation first allowed on research expeditions to Antarctica?

43. Who was the first woman in space? The first American woman in space?

44. Name the women who served as the first female prime ministers in these nations:

Brazil	Iceland
India	Ireland
Israel	New Zealand
Pakistan	The Philippines

45. Who was the first woman to win the Iditarod sled-dog race?

46. Can you name two Hollywood directors who are women?

47. What was the first female rock group to have a Top 40 hit in the U.S.?

48. In what year did a women's bathroom finally have to be added to the Senate building so that newly elected women would not miss the roll call for votes?

49. Name three nations where women were sentenced to death by stoning in 2010.

50. Does the U.S. Constitution have an Equal Rights Amendment?

This isn't an easy test. But it's not your fault if you scored well below an A. If you're like most Americans, women's history simply wasn't part of your education. Even in the twenty-first century, a respectably well-educated person can hold a college degree, plus an advanced graduate degree, and yet know very little about women's contributions to world history beyond the names of a few celebrities and European queens. From kindergarten to medical school, we're taught a curriculum suggesting that important artists, composers, scientists, explorers, and leaders were almost always men.

Interestingly, we don't think of the standard K–12 education as biased—as teaching a limited, one-sided "men's history." It's perceived as "regular" history, maybe boring, but consisting of the standard facts everyone should know. If women aren't mentioned much, maybe it's because they didn't do much in the past—after all, weren't most women just housewives until recently? And anyway, isn't everything fair now?

How we've gone from "most women were just housewives" to "everything's fair now" is a complicated story. Neither of those two statements are correct. It's a myth that women only began having jobs outside the home in the 1970s; throughout history, women have always worked—as servants, as slaves, as prostitutes; in factories, in fields, in sweatshops and mills and taverns; cooking and cleaning for the families of the wealthy, and raising other women's children. But because women were not always paid for their labor, their unwaged work history has been off the record. Because women typically did "women's work" in the homes of others, their services have not always been recognized as skilled labor.

And, despite the ongoing expectation that women will raise families while tending crops, animals, and producing household goods, despite running for office and running for Olympic gold, despite dying as warriors and dying as martyred political prisoners for every cause, most women today still lack the same rights as men. Individual nations may pledge equal rights by law, but local custom prevents that equality from being enforced and enacted—or we wouldn't be waking up daily to a world with honor killings, dowry murder, domestic violence, rape, female circumcision, sex trafficking, sexual harassment, and acid thrown in the face of schoolgirls.

How gender has shaped the course of history is as much a part of our heritage as the development of written language. And the exclusion of women from history books is every bit as political as the demand for full inclusion. *Women's history* writes women back into the record of human achievement, making sure that we learn about our founding mothers, as well as our forefathers' struggles, whatever our culture or national heritage. But that viewpoint—the idea that women are just as important as men—still makes many people uncomfortable.

Chapter One

Why We Don't Learn
Women's History in School

Updating the way that world history is taught presents a real challenge for educational institutions. Despite what you may have heard about colleges being havens for radical faculty, sexism still pervades the halls of academia. A strong ratio of female to male *students* is one kind of statistic; it is not reflected in faculty appointments, where most tenured, full professors are male. This is especially true in history departments, which grant more degrees to men than to women. At the high school/prep school level, it's more common to find men teaching history, and male teachers outnumber females at the annual College Board AP Reading in U.S. History. The AP exam itself primarily asks students to write responsively about men's history and leadership, though this is changing.

Until quite recently, women weren't welcome in higher education, even as students. Their very bodies were restricted to certain schools (women's colleges, religious seminaries, "finishing" schools, teacher-training institutions), certain spaces (women had separate campuses, had to live in specific dormitories with curfews and chaperones), certain majors (nursing, education, English). This meant that women were *not present in the classroom* to advocate for their own inclusion and representation. We can see that this was also true in terms of women's visibility in government and politics, the media, sports, and so forth.

From the late eighteenth century all the way to the late 1970s, the issue of allowing women in higher education created an uproar.[3] Women (and their male allies) fought to allow female students into medical school, law school, and graduate programs. The story of women in American history—and elsewhere—is largely about female *exclusion* from basic institutions like schools. To examine this past is more than just a subject of academic inquiry, or an approach to understanding social change. Women's history is also a cause: an ongoing effort to assure half the world of fair representation in the human record, and to preserve women's memories as truthfully/authentically as possible. For example, girls aspiring to Ivy League colleges today should learn that up until 1969, the smartest women in the world could not apply to Princeton, Harvard, or Yale. And for several years after that, women were only allowed in through a fixed quota system requiring three or four males to be accepted for every female student grudgingly enrolled. (Harvard did not adopt sex-blind admissions until 1976.)

Some critics oppose altering the *academic canon* (traditionally assigned class readings, essential documents penned by men) to include additional coursework, arguing that women's history—

---

[3] Good sources include *College Girls,* by Lynn Peril; *Women of the Republic,* by Linda Kerber; *The Creation of Feminist Consciousness,* by Gerda Lerner; *The Chosen,* by Jerome Karabel; and *To Believe in Women,* by Lillian Faderman.

like black history, Native American studies, etc.—is mere political correctness masquerading as a humanities discipline. Conservative women, too, have contended that more inclusive historical perspectives will just replace the "timeless truths" of Western heritage with a radical agenda. (More on this later.)

Historians, students, archivists, and others in the women's history field believe that a rational and balanced inquiry into the past must include what women were doing at the time, not just men. However, at most institutions of higher learning, women's history is a separate specialty. These courses are not always available to interested students—even at top private schools and colleges. Regrettably, where women's history courses and majors do exist, some faculty advisors discourage bright students from enrolling, scoffing at the value of such coursework.

One may get the sense that the study of women is not just neglected, but downright forbidden. Here are some reasons why women's history is left out of what we learn:

Women's roles stem from religious teachings. To examine women's history is to deconstruct, or take apart, the scriptural teachings on women's status that led to long-lasting attitudes and state laws. Critical reviews of holy religious texts are offensive to many people of faith: Isn't it blasphemy to second-guess what God/Allah/Saint Paul/Confucius intended? Should public schools risk alienating the parents of many different faiths?

Threats to male status. Women's history makes men look bad, and undermines male authority. Powerful male leaders in history, the very men who symbolize human rights and democratic progress, turn out to be wife-beaters, adulterers, or hypocrites who consistently voted down women's rights. (As I write, former California Governor Arnold Schwarzenegger has just revealed that he fathered a child with one of his domestic employees—a woman hired to assist his own wife.)

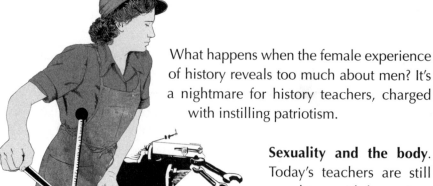

What happens when the female experience of history reveals too much about men? It's a nightmare for history teachers, charged with instilling patriotism.

Sexuality and the body. Today's teachers are still urged to avoid discussions of sex and sexuality in the K–12 classroom; such curricula, if allowed at all, are tightly controlled. Alas, much of women's history is about the nitty-gritty of virginity, chastity, reproduction, and sexual reputation. Would students have to have parental permission to learn women's history? (It may seem funny that parents nonetheless accept their kids being exposed to violence in the movies, videogames, or cartoons, as well as standard history lessons about heroic battles. But plenty of people prefer fictional or glorified violence to material about girls' rights.)

Preserving traditional family roles. The annoyance factor of adding women's history material to a school year already jammed with standardized tests is one thing. But for many conservative parents and educators, it's also an ideological imposition. Beginning in the early 1980s, America's powerful right-wing evangelical lobby began mounting campaigns to preserve *traditional family values* in government, law, and education. Many parents upset with values discussions in the classroom (including open debate on the intended role of women) began home schooling their children. To this day, in Texas, conservative school boards make sure that the textbooks ordered for public schools uphold roles consistent with conservative teachings on the American family. School-board approval wields enormous economic clout in a place like Texas, which places more schoolbook orders than any other state system.

All four of these rationalizations for excluding women's history are interconnected, as we'll see. Basically, looking at and admiring women [the female body] has been forbidden by most religions, so that looking at and admiring *women's history,* too, takes men into problematic terrain. Much of Scripture suggests that women are temptresses, unclean, and dangerous to men. Just consider the problem of Eve. The very first woman—according to the Bible, which informs so much of Western heritage—ruined everything.[4]

Religious Teachings on Women

For Jews and Christians, women's history begins with the appearance of Eve, the first woman, in Genesis. However, sharp-eyed Bible scholars know there are two different creation stories. The earliest passage, Genesis 1:27, suggests that God made male and female at the same time: "male and female he created them." This seems to put both sexes on an equal and even holy basis; both made at the same time, and in the image of God.

Later, Genesis 2:21–23 offers a very different story, telling us that man—or Adam—was created first, formed out of dust. While Adam slept, God took one of Adam's ribs to create a female companion for him, Eve. This version establishes woman as the "second sex," and, importantly, as being created both *from* and *for* man. "She shall be called Woman, because she was taken out of Man." [5]

Many of the negative qualities ascribed to women throughout Western history stem from Adam and Eve's disobedience in the Garden of Eden. Eve, lured by the snake (women are easily led astray by the devil: guard them!), decides to taste the forbidden fruit on the Tree of

---

[4] Jewish tradition has an even scarier first wife for Adam: the willful Lilith.

[5] It's for this reason that some feminists in the 1970s and 80s adopted the spelling *womyn*.

15

Knowledge. (Women are willful and disobedient: punish them! Knowledge will corrupt good women: keep them ignorant!) By disobeying God's command to resist the apple, Eve tempts Adam to sin as well. (Women are the cause of man's downfall; men must not trust women; women should not lead men.)

My student Taylor, raised as a churchgoing Christian, clearly remembers being introduced to this material. "I learned that God was so angry at Eve because she had brought sin into the world. Hearing this for the first time, I remember being excited that there was a girl in the story because Bible stories were mostly about men... But one thing I walked away with was that women were more naïve back then. I knew that *I* would have been able to stick to the rules." Taylor's mixed response, as a child, is understandable: She longed to identify with the female in the story, but refused to accept the premise that all women are naturally naïve or inclined toward disobedience.

In relating God's punishments for Adam and Eve, the Bible establishes clearly different sex roles for men and women. In Genesis 3:17, God tells Adam "Because you have listened to the voice of your wife ... cursed is the ground." Adam will "earn his bread by the sweat of his face" (male = breadwinner); Genesis 3:16 commands Eve to suffer what we still call "the curse" of menstruation and labor pains. "I will greatly multiply your pain in childbirth: In pain you shall bring forth children, yet your desire shall be for your husband, and he shall rule over you." Having demonstrated her need for a tight leash, Eve will forever be controlled by her uterus and her husband. These basic story lines effectively limited women for centuries thereafter; even a desire for education could be seen as a willful girl's quest for that forbidden Tree of Knowledge. As soon as girls were able to menstruate, they were married to husbands who gained complete legal control over their lives.

Both Judaism and Christianity reinforce additional restrictions on women's bodies and minds. Many of these are found in Leviticus, in the Hebrew Bible; for instance, Leviticus chapters 12 and 15 tell us that women are unclean during their menstrual periods, and that this uncleanliness is "catching"; so men, beware! Leviticus 15:19: "When a woman has a discharge of blood which is her regular discharge from her body, she shall be in her impurity for seven days, and whoever touches her shall be unclean … and everything upon which she lies during her impurity shall be unclean; everything also upon which she sits shall be unclean." These blood impurities also applied after childbirth. Significantly, we learn in Leviticus that Moses is to instruct the people of Israel "If a woman conceives, and bears a male child, then she shall be unclean seven days, as at the time of her menstruation, she shall be unclean." On the eighth day, when she is clean and may reemerge in mixed company, her newborn son is circumcised, a ceremony welcoming him into tribal membership. "Then she shall continue for thirty-three days in the blood of her purifying; she shall not touch any hallowed thing, nor come into the sanctuary, until the days of her purifying are completed. But if she bears a female child, then she shall be unclean two weeks, as in her menstruation, and she shall continue in the blood of her purifying for sixty-six days." In other words, the birth of a girl results in double uncleanliness, and is not celebrated with a tribal ritual after the mother completes her seclusion. Eventually, some variations of these customs were incorporated into Christian and Catholic practices; in some eras Catholic women could not receive communion during their periods, and mothers recovering from childbirth were not allowed to be present at a child's baptism.

But consider the math: A woman is kept apart from men and from the sanctuary for two weeks of menstrual impurity. Since Judaism's *tacharos mishpocha* (laws of family purity) allow a wife to have marital relations with her husband only during the two other weeks of the month, when she was most likely to conceive, this guaranteed a high rate of pregnancy—with weeks and months of impurity time after each birth, and each period. On how many days of the year would a Hebrew wife be able to appear in public at all, among men, or touch holy objects? Constant impurity meant she would certainly be unable to fulfill the responsibilities of a rabbi or community leader.

And these customs are far from dead. Jewish law is followed to the letter in today's ultra-Orthodox and Hasidic communities, where contemporary rabbis urge followers to respect *minhag* (religious practices and customs) like these: "Women are permitted to *daven* in *shul* [pray in synagogue] during their menstrual periods. However, they should not look at the *Sefer Torah* [the scroll containing the Five Books of Moses] while it is being raised.... It is also customary not to visit a cemetery during that time.... There is a difference of opinion, though, whether this applies until she has purified herself, or only during the actual period."[6] This author, who published his third edition of *A Guide for the Jewish Woman and Girl* in 1981, adds that the very sight and sound of a woman prevents devout family men from praying: "A man is not permitted to *daven* [pray], recite a *Brocho* [a blessing] or even study Torah [the Hebrew Bible] when facing a woman (including his own wife or daughter) who is not properly covered. It is even questionable if averting his eyes helps.... A girl or a woman should not sing in the presence of men. Even her husband, father, son, or brother may not *daven* or recite a *Brocho* while hearing her singing."[7]

Thus women's spiritual purity is directly connected to physical purity, itself linked to life stages and relationships with men. Since giving birth creates impurity, we read in Job 14: 1–4 that: "Man that is born of a woman is of few days and full of trouble.... Who can bring a clean thing out of an unclean?" This verse has also been translated more starkly as: "How can he be clean that is born of woman?"

The idea that women are *unclean* became a standard justification for their exclusion—from public events to community sites and, even, fields and vineyards. This is by no means limited to Judaism. We also find it in Islam, which tells men: "Let women alone at such times and go not unto them till they are cleansed" (verse 2:222 of the Koran). Many, many cultures from Africa to Indonesia expect women to remain separate from men, from cooking, or from sacred spaces during their periods, sometimes even isolating them in *menstrual huts*. Prohibited activities might include handling money (Bali) or entering temples, cemeteries, or mosques (Malaysia, Kyrgyzstan, the Greek Orthodox, and Zoroastrian faiths) during one's period. Even food preparation—a tradi-

---

[6] Dov Eisenberg, *A Guide for the Jewish Woman and Girl.* Brooklyn: Z. Berman, 1981; p. 152.

[7] Ibid., pp. 140–141.

Dogon Menstrual Hut

tionally female activity—or remaining in the kitchen area of a home may be temporarily forbidden, as in India (for Parsi and Hindu women). And Pliny the Elder, a Roman writing in the first century A.D., declared in his volume *Natural History* that in the presence of a menstruating woman, wine will become sour, seeds will grow sterile, the milk of a pregnant mare will turn sour, knives will grow blunt, grass will wither and die, and much more.[8]

The idea that a menstruating woman is dangerous and unfit for normal domestic tasks shows up in some unexpected places. For instance, a popular folk cookbook published in the U.S. in 1961, the year I was born, contains this information under "How to Make Mayonnaise": "If you are a woman do not attempt to make mayonnaise during menstruating time as the mayonnaise simply will not blend together at all…. This is not superstition but a well-established fact known to all women."[9]

After stressing woman's natural uncleanliness and impurity, the Old Testament turns to community themes of virginity, harlotry, and rape. Women appear over and over in violent, X-rated Bible stories, making today's more progressive Hebrew school students

---

[8] For an interesting source on global menstruation taboos throughout history, check out the online "Museum of Menstruation and Women's Health," a website maintained by one dedicated American man.

[9] George Leonard Herter, *Bull Cook and Authentic Historical Recipes and Practices.* Waseca, Minn: Herter's, Inc., 1963; p. 148.

cringe. In Deuteronomy 22:13, we learn that a bride's virginity may be challenged by a suspicious groom, must then be verified before an entire community (in the ancient custom of displaying the wedding night's bloodied sheets), and if the poor bride did not appear to bleed enough, the entire male population is invited to stone her to death.

If any man takes a wife, and goes in to her, and then spurns her, and charges her with shameful conduct … saying, "I took this woman, and when I came near her, I did not find in her the tokens of virginity," then the father of the young woman and her mother shall take and bring out the tokens of her virginity to the elders of the city in the gate…. And they shall spread the garment before the elders of the city…. But if the thing is true, that the tokens of virginity were not found in the young woman, then they shall bring out the young woman to the door of her father's house, and the men of her city shall stone her to death with stones, because she has wrought folly in Israel by playing the harlot in her father's house.

What about a young virgin girl who is seized and raped? The Bible declares that the rapist has to pay a virgin's father fifty shekels—but then "She shall be his wife, because he has violated her" (Deuteronomy 22:29). This was to prevent a "ruined" girl from being unmarriageable, a form of disgrace as well as an economic liability to her family, but it does set a precedent for permanently handing over the victim to her assailant without her consent. We assume the Bible discusses this situation because it was common, rather than unknown; to this day, young girls in developing countries are most often "seized" when they are sent off alone to do the chores that are considered women's work—collecting water and firewood.

The rape of a virgin girl exacts a penalty, but it's not nearly as horrific as the hint of male rape—male homosexuality is specifically forbidden in Leviticus 20:13. Today, much is made of this religious prohibition against homosexuality, although Leviticus 20 is just as harsh on adulterers, for whom the penalty is also death.

Nevertheless, we get the term *sodomy* from Sodom and Gomorrah, where (in Judges 19:24) the rape of a virgin is offered in lieu of a male-on-male sexual attack. " 'Behold, here are my virgin daughter and his concubine; let me bring them out now. Ravish them and do with them what seems good to you; but against this man do not do so vile a thing. But the men would not listen to him. So the man seized his concubine, and put her out to them; and they knew her, and abused her all night until the morning." How was this ill-used sexual slave then comforted, when she collapsed on her master's threshold at dawn? "He took a knife, and laying hold of his concubine he divided her, limb by limb, into twelve pieces and sent her throughout all the territory of Israel."

There is incestuous violence toward women, too, in 2 Samuel 10–18, where Amnon rapes his sister Tamar: "He took hold of her, and said to her, 'Come lie with me, my sister.' She answered him, 'No, my brother, do not force me; for such a thing is not done in Israel; do not do this wanton folly. As for me, where could I carry my shame?' … but he would not listen to her; and being stronger than she, he forced her, and lay with her. Then Amnon hated her with very great hatred…. And Amnon said to her, 'Arise, be gone.' "

Even the Almighty threatens all the women of Babylon with rape in Isaiah 13:16: "Their houses will be plundered and their wives ravished." For harlots—and witches—the punishment is stoning.

There are depictions of empowered women in the Old Testament, to be sure: Deborah the prophet, Jael who nails Sisera's ear

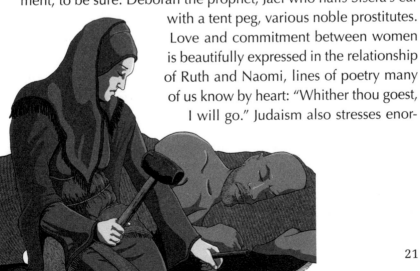

with a tent peg, various noble prostitutes. Love and commitment between women is beautifully expressed in the relationship of Ruth and Naomi, lines of poetry many of us know by heart: "Whither thou goest, I will go." Judaism also stresses enor-

21

mous respect for the motherline by favoring matrilineal ancestry (despite all the emphasis on Moses and Abraham and King David, one inherits one's Jewish identity through Mom). However, the problem of the female body overwhelms these positive examples and images.

Then we come to the New Testament. Here, the negative imagery of Eve meets a fresh counterpart in the virgin motherhood of Mary, and Mary's own immaculate (sinless) conception. Christian feminists point with pleasure to the texts where Jesus invited women as well as men to learn and to preach: "Your sons and your daughters shall prophesy" (Acts 2:17). Christ is portrayed as sympathetic to female prostitutes and as deliberately choosing to affiliate with "unclean" and outcast women.

However, the later gospels attributed to Christ's disciples, particularly Paul, set stern limits on women's public influence and power. The most famous of these passages include Paul's First Letter to the Corinthians 11: "The head of every man is Christ, the head of a woman is her husband," followed by 1 Corinthians 14:34: "The women should keep silence in the churches. For they are not permitted to speak, but should be subordinate, as even the law says. If there is anything they desire to know, let them ask their husbands at home. For it is shameful for a woman to speak in church," and Paul's Letter to the Ephesians 5:22: "Wives, be subject to your husbands, as to the Lord. For the husband is the head of the wife as Christ is the head of the church" (repeated again in his Letter to the Colossians 3:18). I Timothy 2:11–15 finalizes women's proper place in Christianity:

Let a woman learn in silence with all submissiveness. I permit no woman to teach or to have authority over men; she is to keep silent. For Adam was formed first, then Eve; and Adam was not deceived, but the woman was deceived and became a transgressor. Yet woman will be saved through bearing children, if she continues in faith and love and holiness, with modesty.

The first letter of Peter 3–7 concedes that although women are the weaker sex, they can be such good Christian role models that they may end up changing/saving their less pious husbands:

23

Likewise you wives, be submissive to your husbands, so that some, though they do not obey the word, may be won without a word by the behavior of their wives, when they see their reverent and chaste behavior. Let not yours be the outward adorning with braiding of hair, decoration of gold, and wearing of robes, but let it be the hidden person of the heart with the imperishable jewel of a gentle and quiet spirit…as Sarah obeyed Abraham, calling him lord.… Likewise you husbands, live considerately with your wives, bestowing honor on the woman as the weaker sex.

This passage, and that last line of First Timothy 15, set up a kind of code for how women—lacking all other rights—might shape home and society: through motherhood and wifely influence, not through public ostentation or having public authority. Eventually, the options for women within the approved, private sphere of maternal influence grew to include what American educators called *Republican Motherhood,* and what historian Gerda Lerner called *authorization through motherhood.* Some feminist theologians and antislavery activists eventually argued that Galatians 3:28 effectively cancelled out all legal rankings based on gender, race, or national origin: "There is neither male nor female, neither Jew nor Greek, neither slave nor free—all are one, in Jesus." But with an overload of messages requiring women to stay silent, chaste, or, ideally, celibate, women in Christendom found it increasingly immodest to appear in public at all. Their challenge, for the next two thousand years, was regaining the right to preach, teach, and speak before men.

Fundamentalist Christians and Orthodox Jews take the Bible literally as the Word of God, just as devout followers of Islam's *sharia* law use the Koran and its *hadith* (teachings) on women and men to justify traditional gender practices. Throughout history, because most people were neither literate nor wealthy, the Bible might be the only book found in any household—and that's only after the invention of the printing press, the translation of scripture into the vernacular (local languages), and the Protestant Revolution. The inaccessibility of Bible study for average women (and men) until very recently only enhanced the power priests, ministers, and rabbis had to interpret biblical laws for their congregations.

However, the secular viewpoint in academia is that the Bible is also a human text assembled by men, in datable time periods with all their attendant biases. Moreover, the global history of men, women, and civilization itself predates what we know as the written Bible or any Judeo-Christian beliefs. Countless civilizations were already well-organized and thriving throughout Africa, Asia, the Mediterranean, and the Fertile Crescent long *before* Judaism and Christianity developed gender-defining sacred texts. Not every creation story portrayed a male God the Father giving birth to the world; most early cultures practiced *goddess worship,* although restrictions on mortal women could still be seen alongside goddess worship, as in ancient Greece, Babylon, and Sumer.

Traditional Jews and Christians are very nervous about acknowledging *goddess worship.* Its roots are in the ancient world, when the earliest tribal societies observed that all life emerges from the mother, and that females of every species feed their young. Through daily work in agriculture (although *gathering* is never made to seem as important as *hunting*), women also guaranteed human survival by growing, harvesting, and storing most of their community's food. All of these observable realities led to cave-wall art and practices reflecting human belief in a life-giving goddess, millennia before the more familiar God the Father of Judaism, Christianity, and Islam. With the arrival of monotheism, however, goddess worship gave way to faith in a masculine Father God who dominated as the Creator of all life. Female religious leadership became more and more problematic, as women were seen as temptresses leading men to sin. Instead of symbolizing powerful goddess figures, women (and their bodies) appeared more and more as obstacles to male salvation. With the exception of the Virgin Mary, women in religion were gradually limited to auxiliary roles such as nuns, and cloistered in convents, unseen. To aspire to more contradicted Paul's teachings. Today, one of the most bitter debates in theology continues to be whether or not a woman may be a priest or rabbi, rendering learned (and final) decisions in courts of religious law. And panic about goddess worship—easily confused with Wicca, witchcraft, and paganism—is a key reason educators are unhappy teaching women's history that predates

Christianity; listening to witches and wizards is specifically prohibited in Leviticus (that's why many Christian families forbid their children from reading the popular *Harry Potter* books, by the way).

The folk rituals associated with goddess culture may appear as heretical—May pole dances were banned by our Puritans, although in the twentieth century the justification for doing away with May Queen rituals was that May Day had become identified as a Communist holiday. Some women's folkways survived the destruction of goddess worship. But teaching the idea that women may have enjoyed more rights and higher status before Judaism and Christianity set new limits is, for many good-hearted people of faith today, utter blasphemy.

Male Status and Reputation (or, Women's History Makes Men Look Bad)

Male control of women, throughout history, has been physical as well as faith-based. The Bible passages mentioned previously demonstrate that women's history is very much about sexual control, and in too many instances that meant sexual abuse. What we consider basic human rights today—the right to choose your own marriage partner, and to be protected from enslavement, coercive sex, and domestic violence—were rights not granted to previous generations. Certainly, they were not rights available to three specific groups controlled by adult males: children, females of all ages, and servants or slaves.

One reason women's history is still neglected in school is that it sheds an unflattering light on important men. Male leaders—warriors, generals, politicians in positions of power, property owners—were assumed to possess great sexual prowess, and, perhaps, to have "needs" beyond monoga-

26

mous marriage. Throughout history, despite the commandment against adultery, both rich and poor men had access to female sexual companions outside of marriage, a reality shown in the title of one excellent book I teach, Sarah Pomeroy's *Goddesses, Whores, Wives, and Slaves*. These extramarital relationships were allowed, if not praised, due to customs and practices including polygamy and slavery. But sexual congress with young girls, slaves, concubines, and multiple available wives would not be called "moral" by today's standards. The Bible, again, shows that female captives and concubines were routinely exchanged as spoils of war; and of course the story of Sodom of Gomorrah is one of virgin daughters being offered to total strangers as hospitality. Kings 2 tells us that venerable King Solomon the Wise had 1,000 wives: 700 princesses, 300 concubines! Their stories and perspectives are unknown to us. Wise and powerful men, and victorious warriors, were often rewarded with the bonus of multiple partners; in contrast, we hear almost no anecdotes about a ruling queen with 1,000 husbands.

In early American history, one of the great controversies concerns our slave-owning Founding Fathers. I teach at a university named for the first American President, George Washington. Most children in the U.S. are taught that Washington was so honest he could not tell a lie. What happens to a student's regard for George Washington when teachers, too, are honest, and reveal that George owned slaves—that, in the starkest terms, he bought and sold women?

Only recently have we examined the Colonial past from the viewpoint of Sally Hemmings, Thomas Jefferson's slave and mistress, the not-so-secret mother of his children. Their relationship may have included some genuinely romantic elements, yet it was burdened with inequalities and scandal, secrecy and denial. Today, the descendents of Hemmings and Jefferson struggle to have their ancestry recognized and validated. And some of them sit in elementary school classrooms where they are guaranteed to learn only about Jefferson, and not Hemmings. This is but one example of why "women's history" is considered too controversial a legacy for schoolchildren. As a slave woman, Sally Hemmings was entitled to none of the new freedoms outlined in the U.S. Constitution, a document written, at least in part, by the father of her children.

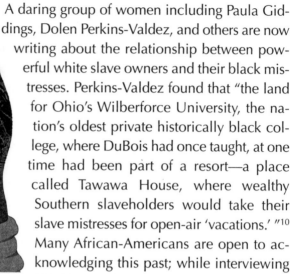

A daring group of women including Paula Giddings, Dolen Perkins-Valdez, and others are now writing about the relationship between powerful white slave owners and their black mistresses. Perkins-Valdez found that "the land for Ohio's Wilberforce University, the nation's oldest private historically black college, where DuBois had once taught, at one time had been part of a resort—a place called Tawawa House, where wealthy Southern slaveholders would take their slave mistresses for open-air 'vacations.' "[10] Many African-Americans are open to acknowledging this past; while interviewing Perkins-Valdez for *The Washington Post,* reporter Lonnae O'Neal Parker learned that "When she explained that the book was about black slave mistresses and their owners, a Smithsonian museum guard said, 'Oh, like my great-grandmother.' " [11]

Where famous men had other sexual quirks, there's even more silence. Playwright Carolyn Gage is one scholar who has been unafraid to examine incest in the nineteenth century, most recently in *Speak Fully the One Awful Word.* She explains, "That one awful word was 'incest,' and Harriet Beecher Stowe was referring to Lord Byron's incestuous relations with his half-sister, as witnessed by Byron's wife. Stowe was as vilified for exposing Lord Byron as she had been lionized for writing *Uncle Tom's Cabin….* She specifically repudiated the prevailing Christian ethos that encouraged wives to suffer in silence for the sake of protecting the family."

Sexuality

By now it's apparent that much of women's history is very, very intimate. Within the private sphere, a daughter's virginity was closely guarded until her betrothal and marriage; rape or any other interference with female honor brought shame to an entire tribe.

---

[10] Lonnae O'Neal Parker, "A Tender Spot in Master-Slave Relations." *Washington Post,* January 23, 2011; p. E3.

[11] Ibid.

Victims endured blame, not compassion; they might be put on trial, put to death, or simply forced to marry the rapist. The question of "honor" followed women across time, faith, and geography; *honor killings* took root as a brutal practice in much of Middle East culture, flourishing as a custom of tribal order well after the rise of Judaism and Islam. In modern times, as a visitor to Iraqi in 1968 wrote, "When a girl is born ... people say to her parents, 'May Allah be kinder to you next time'—not because the infant is not loved, but because she may someday disgrace the family."[12]

This silencing of the victim's viewpoint allowed the *double standard* to flourish. Men were not expected to be virgins at marriage. (How could such a test even be administered?) In contrast, traditional communities and cultures use various "tests" to determine if a young bride bled on her wedding night, with a maze of laws and penalties surrounding this ritual. But it was never a moral concern alone. Proof of virginity was also the last step in a financial transaction: the transfer of a girl from one man (father) to another (husband). In her interviews with rural Afghan women, Isabelle Delloye noted: "The young girl's virginity on the wedding night is the guarantee of undefiled motherhood. If the bride should not be a virgin, she will be sent back immediately to her father and the money spent for the wedding will be reclaimed ... but in reality the occasion almost never presents itself. And if the betrothed pair should have committed an indiscretion before the wedding, a pigeon's blood will be used to stain the sheet."[13] Similar customs prevailed in Morocco, where sympathetic female friends or even the bridegroom might secretly substitute a sheep membrane, or pigeon or rooster's blood to stain the nuptial sheet.[14] Describing these rituals in her book *Sacred Performances*, M. E. Combs-Schilling notes: "No one I know ever witnessed a girl sacrificed.... Past and present, the actual slaying of a bride whose hymen did not bleed has been rare. Yet, the voicing of the possibility takes its toll on females, for it boldly inserts that possibility

[12] Harry G. Nickles, *Middle Eastern Cooking*. New York: Time-Life Books, 1969; p. 110.

[13] Isabelle Delloye, *Women of Afghanistan*. Ruminator Books, 2003; p. 39.

[14] M. E. Combs-Schilling, *Sacred Performances*. New York: Columbia University Press, 1989; p. 209.

into lived existence. The practice exists as a speech act even if not as a physical act."[15] Girls throughout history thus lived in fear of capital punishment for a broken hymen—a very effective means of controlling their participation in mixed-sex or athletic activities. (In the U.S., both horseback and bicycle riding were frowned on in the nineteenth century, as were gynecological exams in the early twentieth, and in the years after World War II, newly available packaged tampons were rejected by many families worldwide as a possible threat to the intact hymen.)[16]

A virgin daughter might bring a high bride-price from a worthy groom—or, depending on custom, require a substantial dowry from her parents at marriage. Either way, the birth of a daughter led families to groan in worry. How would they provide for her? How much attention would be spent on safeguarding her virtue? So much might go wrong, and in the end, after all that worry and care, the girl would vanish into another man's tribe and take on his family name (in China, one popular saying continues to be "Raising a daughter is like watering someone else's plant"). *Dowry murders* in India threaten to overwhelm an already burdened police bureaucracy. But though it is the most important aspect of female identity/property value, and though it was debated and discussed publicly in ancient law, virginity isn't the sort of female "achievement" schoolchildren discuss—except during abstinence-only sex-ed classes.

To be sure, Christian schoolchildren are familiar with the role of the *Virgin Mary,* and casually sing Christmas carols about *the Blessed Virgin* at school pageants; but the anatomical and historic meaning of this term isn't fully articulated at holiday time!

Parents who argue that sexuality has no place in an elementary school lesson tend to forget how often the word *virgin* appears already; in catechism, geography references to virgin land, Virginia, etc. But this is just one example of the embarrassment surrounding women's history. Can a teacher address how women and girls lived in the past without invoking the marriage bed? Throughout much of history, a woman *was* her body—a dangerous equation.

---

[15] Ibid., p. 208.

[16] See Joan Jacobs Brumberg, *The Body Project.*

Even studying something "safe" like fashion, and the history of dress codes, brings us right back to the subject of male arousal.

For instance, because women were held accountable for male temptation, it was incumbent upon them to dress modestly, avert their eyes from the male gaze, and not attract attention from strangers. Depending upon region and custom, this has ranged from a simple hair-cover to a full *burqa*. Hair is a key problem (Saint Paul suggests that hair is a woman's glory and then, simultaneously, recommends that a woman cover her head).[17] Orthodox Judaism ultimately developed the practice of having married women wear wigs or scarves over shorn heads, and Catholic women had to cover their heads in church until the liberalization of such practices after the Vatican II reforms in the 1960s.

Upholding virginity and honor by separating women from public sight altogether resulted in *purdah*, or seclusion. In desert tribal practices, the term *harem* does not mean the number of womenfolk a man has, but actually refers to the portioned section of the tent behind which the female members of the family live and eat. Often, elite women in Roman and early Muslim caliphates were guarded by eunuchs—men guaranteed not to become aroused (or to impregnate the women in their care).

In addition, not only the sight of a woman but the sound of her voice has been a source of temptation to men; this is a theme across time and culture. In ancient Greek mythology, the voices of the Sirens drove men mad; in Judaism, the *kol isha*, or woman's voice, is so arousing that men and women may not sing together. In medieval convent life, female composers and nuns who arranged sacred music might stage concerts for one another, but a male audience could only hear music performed by men. To avoid the problem of using actual female voices and bodies onstage, both Eastern and Western civilizations auditioned young men to act and sing as women. In Rome, young males with beautiful singing voices were castrated before their voices deepened; they trained for the famous *castrati* choirs. In traditional Chinese

---

[17] See Constance Parvey, "The Theology and Leadership of Women in the New Testament," in *Religion and Sexism*, ed. Rosemary Radford Ruether. New York: Simon & Schuster, 1974.

opera and Japanese Kabuki theatre, men played all roles. These solutions preserved female modesty by banning women from appearing before strange men, but allowed men to enjoy the arts and to see representation of the "female" without the possibility of violating custom.

Keeping women out of public performance—and out of public life—meant they would avoid the danger of a *bad reputation*. But the result might be an entire sex with no reputation at all; a history of careful anonymity. Some families still uphold the belief that a woman's name should appear in print only three times in her life: at birth, marriage and death.

Traditional Family Values

Finally, a key reason women's history has not gradually filled our schoolbooks is that many powerful education lobbyists oppose it—and oppose any positive references to the impact of American feminism on opportunities for women. Depictions of powerful women in history who appear to deviate from biblical ideals of womanhood are interpreted as an attack on *traditional family values* by Christian fundamentalist groups—many of which are supported by political appointees in high places. Pat Robertson, the founder of Regent University, is perhaps most famous for his succinct quote: "The feminist agenda is not about equal rights for women. Feminism is a socialist, antifamily, political movement that encourages women to leave their husbands, kill their children, practice witchcraft, destroy capitalism, and become lesbians." Wow! This line first appeared in a 1992 fund-raising letter opposing Iowa's state equal-rights amendment proposal. (Today, Robertson's followers and others opposed to equal rights for women may order T-shirts with this slogan from RightWingStuff.com and other companies advertising "Christian" shirts.) Speaking on his *700 Club* program in 1991, Robertson declared that Planned Parenthood "is teaching kids to fornicate, to have adultery, every kind of bestiality, homosexuality, lesbianism—everything that the Bible condemns." Similar statements equating women's organizations with Biblical blasphemy created an ongoing dilemma for historians trying to address feminism as an *historical movement* worthy of note in textbooks.

"Feminism is a socialist, anti-family, political movement that encourages women to leave their husbands, kill their children, practice witchcraft, destroy capitalism and become lesbians."

Beginning in the 1970s, evangelical activists organized to charge teachers with promoting *secular humanism,* an approach to social history they perceived as *anti-Christian* and *antifamily.* Loading local school boards with parents and preachers dedicated to keeping feminist ideas out of the classroom, groups such as Educational Research Analysts created a textbook-approval process with strict scrutiny for traditional sex roles: husband as breadwinner, wife in the home. Mel and Norma Gabler were the husband-and-wife team who founded this nonprofit group, which for decades wielded fantastic control over the curriculum students might learn in Texas; though the Gablers have passed on, the Texas school board recently adopted an entire new platform of language and values for its history texts. According to the *Education Reporter,* one of the last acts of "textbook reform" successfully initiated by the Gablers in 2004 required textbook publishers "to define marriage as a lifelong union between a man and a woman instead of referring generically to 'married partners.' "[18] Images of women living apart from men, or foregoing children to have careers, threatened the family.

Neither of the Gablers had college degrees, but their power to veto the adoption of state textbooks led some publishers to send

[19] David P. Gushee, "The Palin Predicament," in *USA Today,* September 15, 2008. Gushee's column raised the interesting question of whether religious conservatives could support the candidacy of Sarah Palin.

drafts for their approval rather than risk being dropped from the list of "approved" schoolbooks in Texas and California. Evolution, sex education, disrespect for authority (for instance, any criticism of the United States for its institution of slavery), and emphasis on the contributions of minorities were particularly problematic for the Gablers (and their followers in other states). The result of such trends in education guaranteed that public schools, and to a certain extent parochial schools, could not represent new research on women's history without risking backlash from con-

"Until textbooks are changed, there is no possibility that crime, violence, veneral disease and abortion rates will decrease."

servative watchdog groups—and these grew apace during the 1980s and 90s, buoyed by talk radio and programs such as Reverend Jerry Falwell's *Old Time Gospel Hour* and Pat Roberston's *700 Club*. Through the media of television, radio, and internet, citizens who had never encountered a women's history class or textbook could nevertheless be mobilized to campaign in protest against students' exposure to this field of scholarship.

Opposition to various kinds of female empowerment had increased after 1987, during which the fundamentalist Council on Biblical Manhood and Womanhood (CBMW) clarified roles for Christian women and men in America: "God's plan is for men to serve as godly leaders in home and church, and for women to accept a complementary role in voluntary submission to male authority."[19] In 1998, the Southern Baptist Convention passed a resolution urging wives to submit to their husbands and to accept the principle of male headship. A women's history lesson plan celebrating female authority over men would contradict these be-

---

[18] *Education Reporter,* December 2004.

34

liefs. Most recently, in 2009, the Texas Board of Education reaffirmed strict standards for history and social-studies texts and requested that references to Anne Hutchinson be removed. One report from these proceedings noted that "Peter Marshall, an evangelical minister who also advocated for stronger emphasis on the role of Christianity in U.S. history, dismissed Hutchinson, saying 'She was certainly not a significant Colonial leader, and didn't accomplish anything except getting herself exiled from the Massachusetts Bay Colony for making trouble.' "[20]

Future generations may never hear of the robust troublemaking women who were their foremothers in struggle as advocates for freedom. And so, for all of the reasons explored in this first chapter, most of us are denied full access to *women's history* in school.

Anne Hutchinfon 1591- 1643

---

[20] National Women's History Museum website; reprinted from Jone Johnson Lewis, "Women Making Trouble," July 30, 2009.

Chapter Two

A Basic Walking Tour Through the Past

Nice country... we'll take it.

How is an introductory course in *women's history* taught? There are as many approaches to women's history as there are women in the world.

The way an individual woman might become known as "important," "a good wife," or even a "bad woman" of course depended on where and when she lived. Her opportunities, responsibilities, and limitations were based on local customs and laws. The recorded history of women in Japan does not tell us the same story as the history of women in Macedonia, or Madagascar, or Tonga, or Iran, or New York City. But in trying to collapse the history of all women in the world into one neat story line, Western historians created an obvious bias towards European history, addressing the progress of prominent Christian nations and famous events or individuals from the Western hemisphere (and what is called the *global North*). This approach is grossly unrepresentative of regal African, Asian, Arab, Pacific Islander, and indigenous woman of all lands, too many of whom not only dealt with the gender codes established by men of their own tribal cultures, but also colonization by Western powers—usually unwelcome male occupiers with racist beliefs about "native" women.

Thankfully, today's teachers and students can choose from an enormous range of research on women in every nation, research collected and written *by* local women rather than constructed top-down by male anthropologists (American, English, German, French, etc). Still, generalized approaches to women's history tend to move gradually from the ancient world of the Middle East and Mediterranean up into Christianized Europe, following a trajectory of excavated sites like Catal Huyuk in Turkey, the caves of south Germany, and Ceide Fields or Achill Island in Ireland, all of which have yielded rich depictions of women's lives. Historians then take us outward from Europe via the Age of Exploration by European men like Columbus—men whose "discoveries" and claims of "new" lands regrettably led to acts of war and genocide against indigenous tribes, plus enslaving and trading African women in Spanish, Portuguese, Dutch, British, French, and Belgian colonies. When black, white and indigenous women finally began to gain access to education and could present their own demands, Western educational institutions and archives still tended to value, publish, or otherwise preserve what "proper" [affluent, white] women did, wrote, or thought. Globally, the experiences of illiterate, impoverished women on society's margins were seldom recorded for others to learn from. Instead, the oral tradition of song and story lines, as well as crafts, transmitted rich information from mother to daughter, down through generations of struggle.

My own years as a student were certainly shaped by these biases and conditions of scholarship. And I soon learned that the central ideas and laws governing American women's "proper place" went all the way back, in a reverse timeline, to certain sex roles and attitudes we Americans borrowed from English law, European Christianity (both Catholic and Protestant), government philosophies of the Enlightenment and ancient Greece and Rome, and class systems—all limiting the way women accessed property, wages, knowledge, and marriage rights.

This chapter offers just one approach for a contemporary American student (or reader) to grasp *what came before* the more equal citizenship status women enjoy today. Looking at key points from the Western heritage is a sort of walking tour through major women's history moments. Chapter Three will then offer ten additional, topic-based approaches to understanding women's history, including on-going controversies about who/what should be included.

In my own survey course at George Washington University, where I usually enroll about 120 first-year students each fall, we simply begin at the dawn of time—in *prehistory*, with cavewomen.

The Paleolithic Cavewoman

Most of us are familiar with comic-strip images of busty cavewomen being dragged by their hair as the earliest references to gendered life. A more respectful approach acknowledges that 40,000 years ago, the earliest women we know of were worshipped for their life-giving abilities. Before the written word could preserve the thoughts of ancient peoples, cave art and carvings represented their daily human concerns.

And these oldest carved figurines show utter awe for woman's fertility, her sexual body, and her physical ability to reproduce and then feed children.

One of the oldest human bodies known to science is that of a female, a mostly complete skeleton (*Australopithecus afarensis*) found in Ethiopia in 1974. This fossil of an ancient woman, discovered by Don Johanson, was nicknamed "Lucy" by the team of scientists who happened to be listening to the Beatles hit "Lucy in the Sky With Diamonds" in their campground. One estimate is that she might have lived three million years ago, well before early humans invented stone tools (in the Paleolithic Era, or Old Stone Age). More recently, in 2008 archaeologist Nicholas Conard found the ivory figurine of a Paleolithic female in a cave of southwestern Germany called Hohle Fels, dating back to at least 35,000 years ago. Carved with a ring where her head should be, possibly to be worn as jewelry, this figure is provocative to our twenty-first-century eyes. In the journal *Nature,* archaeology reporter Paul Mellars wrote "And the figure is explicitly—and blatantly—that of a woman, with an exaggeration of sexual characteristics (large, projecting breasts, a greatly enlarged and explicit vulva, and bloated belly and thighs) that by twentieth-century standards could be seen as bordering on the pornographic." [21]

Even better known than the Lucy skeleton or that ivory figurine is the popular discovery called the Venus of Willendorf. Dating back approximately 25,000 years, discovered in Austria in 1908, this late Paleolithic figure is a perfectly intact statue—unlike Lucy and the Hohle Fels Venus. The Willendorf statue has a head, but no face—her sexual characteristics were what mattered most to the artist, reflecting the values of the time. What mattered was whether a woman could reproduce, and breast-feed.

The ancient figures of women who appear pregnant, lactating, or sexually potent suggest that our earliest ancestors truly valued female fertility and saw it as worthy of recognition in totems and spiritual art. Did early humans understand how women became pregnant? The mystery of just how men "made babies" might be un-

---

[21] Paul Mellars, *Nature,* v. 459, 14 May 2009; p. 176.

clear, but everyone knew that life came out of the female body—
and that a newborn could nurse, immediately, from the mother's
milk. Some scholars who have studied teeth and bones believe it
was common for children in the ancient world to breastfeed for
many years, so long as their mother remained healthy. Very late
weaning meant two important things: one, those strong and skilled
women who might have *wished* to join the hunts and activities we
think of as "male" were physically tied to children—plus, their bodily fluids could more easily be scented by animals. This kept women
closer to home as *gatherers*. And, two, both male and female humans grew up with the association of the mother as nurturer—a literal source of food. It's not startling that the earliest excavated
images of women portray worship of the female body—a body
shown as fat, healthy, with giant breasts. A *skinny* mother with
empty breasts spelled doom for hungry children and the future fertility of the entire tribe—quite unlike our modern fashion prefer-
ences for stick-thin, decidedly unmaternal-looking celebrities. Yet
note how we react to a voluptuous, natural image. The very depic-
tion of a healthy nude woman, even in *Nature,* seems pornographic.

The Neolithic Era

As communities settled, domesticated animals, invented tools, and
grew more secure, several important trends changed the fate of
women in the ancient world. Women's fertility became a *commodity* that could be controlled: stolen (women in peaceful set-
tlements might be kidnapped and raped by more aggressive
invaders), traded (in arranged marriages between groups), or
awarded (women could be given as gifts to male allies or to pacify
male enemies). Even the story of the founding of ancient Rome is
one of mass rape. When there weren't enough women, men re-
sorted to raids. In short, rape became a tool of invasion—a
woman's body could literally be invaded, binding her eventual
children to the enemy invader and shifting alliances by force.

As the male role in reproduction became better understood
(breeding animals helped everyone figure out how "mating" led to
increased flocks), we see a shift away from the dynamic fertility of
women to the all-important sperm. In fact, the creative power of

women to give life, one of their most unique powers, was gradually appropriated by men—or subordinated to man's power to *take life* through battle, plunder, even rape.

Both Gerda Lerner and Riane Eisler discuss these shifts in their books on how woman's fertility passed into male control. Eisler's book *The Chalice and the Blade* looks at peaceful societies, such as Crete around 6000 B.C.E., which operated on an egalitarian or partnership model, and where artwork and buildings depicted women's significant roles. With invasions by more warlike tribes during the Bronze Age, Eisler argues, came the need for defensive *weapons* (the "blade" in her book title), as well as new interest in protecting (or restricting) women by building fortifications around exposed settled communities. Gradually, we see a shift from kin-based to class-based social structure, with the most powerful men at the top. And because women were understood to be valuable (all that fertility!), their freedoms became more and more restricted—usually more so if they belonged to elite families. Slaves and servant women, of course, had to go out and about in order to do the daily errands of the elite.

In *The Creation of Patriarchy,* Gerda Lerner, like Eisler and other historians, is careful to avoid suggesting that an earlier system of *matriarchy* existed first. Just because women had high status didn't mean that men's status was low, or that women once ruled over all men the way many religious hierarchies and governments eventually consisted of men ruling over women. *Patriarchy* can be seen taking root in the earliest ancient states once societies adopt *hierarchies* with ranked classes of people. Systems with a human hierarchy of slaves, servants, wives, and kings allowed for the growing acceptance of what Eisler calls a *dominator model*—male dominating over female, rich over poor, masters over slaves, and so on. Eisler explains the difference between a matriarchy, with powerful women subjugating men, and what we do find archaeologically: "… the other alternative for human organization: a partnership society in which neither half of humanity is ranked over the other and diversity is not equated with inferiority or superiority."[22] She argues that only after a time of equal partnering did it become normal to see, and justify, one group controlling another—often brutally.

What's confusing to modern students is that even as women gradually lost rights or freedoms in settled communities ruled by strong men, people continued to worship goddesses or female fertility in their spiritual practices. Lerner states, "Long after women are sexually and economically subordinated to men, they still play active and respected roles in mediating between humans and gods as priestesses, seers, diviners, and healers."[23] A book with a nice provocative title is Merlin Stone's *When God Was a Woman*, still in use in women's history courses, offering an archaeological overview of woman's goddess-based religious practices in the ancient world. Stone's collection *Ancient Mirrors of Womanhood: A Treasury of Goddess and Heroine Lore From Around the World* is another fantastic guidebook to the ancient past. We can see that both men and women lived with a sense of the divine female, and the idea that Earth itself is a mother has lasted in most languages. To this day, even the most devout Christian weatherman sometimes refers to "Mother Nature" on the evening news, unaware he is honoring the divine feminine on live national television.

Some Thoughts About Goddess Worship

Goddesses and goddess worship have been found everywhere on planet Earth, from southern Africa to what is today Finland; from Peru to Hawaii to India. Every culture had a female Mother Goddess well before the gradual takeover by male gods and, eventually, the Father-Creator/Lord/King model of monotheism in Judaism, Christianity and Islam. Those interested in goddess history of the ancient

---

[22] Riane Eisler, *The Chalice and the Blade*. San Francisco: Harper & Row, 1988; p. 28.

[23] Gerda Lerner, *The Creation of Patriarchy*. New York: Oxford University Press, 1986; p. 9.

world can explore a gigantic record of art, symbols, and beliefs. A very short list might include:

- Tauert, the mother goddess of ancient in Egypt; and Isis, just as powerful;
- Ishtar (or Inanna), an armed Mesopotamian goddess;
- Astarte, a West Semitic goddess of love and war;
- The many goddesses of ancient Greece: Gaia, the Earth Mother; Athena, patron of power and warfare; Aphrodite, the goddess of love; Hera, patron of women and marriage; Hestia, goddess of home and hearth; Artemis, the Virgin Hunter, goddess of nature and the hunt; Hecate, goddess of witchcraft; Demeter, Earth goddess of grain and agriculture;
- In ancient Rome, Diana, the fertility goddess; Minerva, goddess of war; Juno, guardian of women, and Venus, the goddess of love;
- Lakshmi, wife of Vishnu, India's goddess of good fortune; the warrior goddess Durga, and the destructive goddess Kali;
- Pele, the goddess of the volcano on Mount Kilauea in Hawaii;
- Kuan Yin, in China, and Chang O, goddess of the moon;
- Oya and Oshun, water goddesses of the Yoruba in Nigeria;
- Anansi, the spider goddess of Ghana;
- Baba Yaga, in Russia;
- Kunapipi, the mother goddess of aboriginal Australia;
- Hine, in Polynesia;

- Spider Woman of the Navajo;
- Ix Chel, the Mayan moon goddess; and the Aztec Teteoinnan;
- Ragana, in Lithuania and Latvia, and the Norse goddess Freyja;
- Celtic Brigit; the death goddess Morrigan; and the guardian goddess Eriu—for whom Ireland (Eire) is named.

In Marija Gimbutas' important book *The Language of the Goddess,* she notes that "Goddess-centered art with its striking absence of images of warfare and male domination reflects a social order in which women as heads of clans or queen-priestesses played a central part."[24] But Gimbutas, Eisler, and Lerner agree that with the invasion by more violent clans, a focus on armaments, patrilineal inheritance, and the passing of power or goods from father to son eclipsed the nurturing power of women. Virginity became proof that a girl had been "protected" from invasion, and the role of protector was increasingly assigned to her male family members and guardians. Gradually, goddess worship was replaced by images of all-powerful, destructive, and protective male gods, and, finally, by God the Father, creator of life.

Who Were the Amazons?
It's clear that the male role as warrior had a good bit to do with establishing male superiority as the rule of law in ancient civilizations.

------

[24] Marija Gimbutas, *The Language of the Goddess.* San Francisco: Harper & Row, 1989; p. xx.

Were there female warriors? Yes: the Amazons, who are referenced throughout ancient Greek history and art. The famous Parthenon of Athens included an aspect of heritage that has fascinated the world for centuries: "In the sculpted panels (metopes) on the western end of the temple—the side first visible upon approach—appeared the battle between the

ETRUSCAN AMAZON circa 600 bce

Greeks and Amazons, mythical warrior women who lived at the boundaries of the civilized world free of men and male domination."[25] The very name *Amazon* means "without breast"—*a mazos*. Supposedly, mounted upon horses (unheard of for women!), the Amazons cut off their right breasts to gain a better pull on bow and arrow weaponry. The Amazons spoke a language men could not understand, reared only female children, and—in a reversal of the sex roles of the time—apparently captured men for sexual pleasure. Taming the feisty Amazons became a test for heroic men; in *Goddesses, Whores, Wives, and Slaves,* historian Sarah Pomeroy recounts an ancient scavenger hunt: "One of Hercules' labors was to obtain the girdle of an Amazon queen."[26]

Sumer and Babylon

While ancient Europe struggled to preserve Earth-based goddess culture in the face of armed invasions, the first written laws emerged in Sumer and Babylonia (today, the region of Iraq) around 3500 B.C.E. As Helga Harriman describes, some Sumerian women served as prostitutes—including priestesses. Ordinarily, "Through-

---

[25] Marilyn Katz, "Daughters of Demester: Women in Ancient Greece." In *Becoming Visible,* ed. Renate Bridenthal, Susan Mosher Stuard and Merry Wiesner. Houghton Mifflin, 1998; p. 48.

[26] Pomeroy, p. 24.

UR-SHUBAD of SUMERIA circa 2600 BCE

out the ancient Near East, harlots were usually treated as outcasts: They were required to dress so that they could be distinguished from respectable women and could not cover their heads or wear veils in public."[27] Temple priestesses who had ritual sex as a means of uniting with the Divine were highly regarded; but the dress code for plain harlots reveals that the Middle Eastern practice of "good" women covering their heads was already in place over 5,500 years ago.

During the reign of King Hammurabi, a major legal code created around 1760 B.C.E. demonstrated how women's sexual behavior determined their fate in a settled community. The Code of Hammurabi had about 282 laws—73 of which outlined rules for women. Unhappily, a woman accused of adultery could only prove her innocence by throwing herself into the river. On the other hand, a man who raped another man's fiancée was put to death. One right women enjoyed was divorce. However, children belonged to the father; the laws show that men controlled wives, daughters, and sons. (When divorce first became permitted in the United States, it was customary for the father to gain custody, contrary to practices that now favor the mother. Divorced women, far more than divorced males, have long been considered failed and dangerous females—unfit for motherhood, remarriage, or decent society.)

Egyptian Queens and Pharaohs

Egypt gave civilization much more than the pyramids. For centuries, women there ruled as (or with) pharaohs, the throne passed through the female line, and people worshipped the mother goddess Nut and the goddess Isis (sometimes referred to as "throne woman"). Fifteen hundred years before Christ, Hatshepsut ruled Egypt as a pharaoh; statues show her dressed in the clothes of a

[27] Helga Harriman, *Women in the Western Heritage,* p. 24.

male monarch. Later, around 1365 B.C.E., Nefertiti wielded power in lieu of her ailing husband. Women had rights in Egyptian society that Greek and Roman women could only envy: they were midwives and lawyers, worked outside the home alongside men, enjoyed the right of divorce, and they appear in art as respected public figures. There was actually a medical school for women at the Temple of Neith in Egypt hundreds of years before Christ. Yet females would not be permitted to attend medical school in the United States for another *four thousand years*.

The Israelites

If you've ever attended a Passover seder, you know that life in Egypt was not kind to the enslaved Hebrews, who (led by Moses) escaped to the so-called Promised Land and there received the Ten Commandments. The development of Jewish law, beginning with Adam and Eve and onward to strictly defined roles for women, has already been addressed in Chapter One's tour of the Torah (the Old Testament). In fleeing Egypt's Pharaohs, by 1200 B.C.E. the ancient Hebrews had developed monotheism with a male prophet (Moses), a Father Creator (Yahweh), an archaic story of faith and sacrifice centered around the father and son bond (Abraham's willingness to sacrifice Isaac), and a physical rite of tribal belonging located in the male organ (circumcision). Women were barely involved as rulers or lawmakers, let alone empowered as goddesses.

Many modern feminists have conveniently blamed Judaism for replacing goddess worship once and for all with a code of values entirely controlled by male authorities and a male Creator. This complex argument is investigated by Jewish feminist scholars such as Judith Plaskow, author of *Standing Again at Sinai*. But it's important to mention that there were temple priestesses as well as stoic foremothers in the Bible: Sarah, Rachel, Hannah, Rebecca, Ruth and Naomi, Miriam, Esther, Deborah. Helga Harriman reminds us that the range of roles women actually carried out in their daily lives is attested in the famous Proverbs 31, "A woman of valor, who can find? For her price is above rubies," still chanted as a tribute of respect toward wives by observant Jewish men (in Hebrew, it's *"Aishes chayil, mi imtzo?"*). In Proverbs 31, we learn that a capable wife bought and sold land, harvested, worked in the marketplace, and moved capably between the public and private spheres.[28] Gradually, after the destruction of the Temple in 70 C.E. and the scattering of the Jewish people into the *diaspora* of other lands, Judaism developed a culture of survival almost reversing what we think of as traditional sex roles: the ideal for a pious male was to spend his days in study, perpetuating religious knowledge and scholarship; women, in contrast, while kept out of the top echelons of learning, were respected as breadwinners for these scholarly husbands. Much of later Jewish history, however, is the story of legal oppression in foreign lands, so it's difficult to know which roles Jewish men might have pursued were they not forbidden to own land, serve in militaries, or choose other banned occupations. The stereotype of the tough, outspoken, capable Jewish mother emerged partly as a result of ongoing persecution and hardship.

Less known but significant in Jewish mythology is the story of Lilith, a figure believed to be the first woman even before Eve, but so uppity and willful that she was banished as Adam's companion. She is a demon in the eyes of the pious, but her refusal to submit to male authority has made her a favorite of spiritual rebels. In the 1990s, the feminist concert tour *Lilith Fair* was named after this legendary wildwoman—prompting at least one powerful Christian fundamentalist, the Reverend Jerry Falwell, to generate a letter warning parents to keep their daughters away from Lilith Fair.[29]

---

[28] Harriman, pp. 40-41.

[29] J.M. Smith, "Parents Alert," *National Liberty Journal,* June 1999.

Ancient Greece and Sappho

Greece remained *polytheistic* until well after the arrival of Christianity. Here we find some amazing contradictions. Goddesses were entrenched, defining aspects of civilization: Hecate, Artemis, Athena, Gaia, Aphrodite, Demeter, the Muses. Yet Greek mythology also offers a creation story very similar to the Old Testament's warning about Eve: the legend of Pandora's box. Warned not to give in to her feminine curiosity, defiant Pandora opens a forbidden box, releasing all the trouble in the world to plague men. The similarity to Eve's fall from grace is pretty striking: A woman's curiosity, her desire for knowledge, is a negative force.

Among ordinary mortals, Greek life shows surprising contempt for women. Some historians argue that despite goddess worship, ordinary Greek men feared the female body and found it distasteful (see Philip Slater's *The Glory of Hera*). Statues proclaimed the beauty of the male body—and a very significant shift in the attitude about birth can be seen in the story of Athena, said to be born fully formed from the forehead of Zeus. This is a clear example of the Father-God as creator of life replacing the image of woman, and her womb, as the giver of life. It also shows the social value placed on the male intellect—the head—while women were more or less excluded from learning, and the female body shunned altogether as inferior, problematic, and worse. The philosopher Aristotle believed that women were actually deformed men, suffered from a "wandering womb," and merely incubated babies. The term *hysteria,* later popularized by Sigmund Freud and ultimately contributing the medical term *hysterectomy,* is a Greek word resulting from Aristotle and others' belief that women were at the mercy of their unstable uterus.

"Women oppose change, receive passively, and add nothing of their own."

Sigmund Freud, in: "The Psychical Consequences of the Anatomic Distinction Between the Sexes." 1925.

Under Greek law, women had no political rights. Any property (or dowry) they brought to a marriage was controlled by the husband, and no woman could take action independent of male authority. Only vestal virgins, young priestesses who dedicated their lives to goddess temples in Greece and Rome, could live apart from men. The utter limitation of women according to law, and wealthy families' reliance on slaves, are two attributes of Greece's model "democracy" later reappearing in the early United States. Interestingly, Greek women had slightly more freedom in the warring state of Sparta, where they were permitted exercise (and ate better) to strengthen their fitness as mothers of future warriors. Sparta is an excellent model for examining the mixed message women have received throughout history: giving birth to a son is woman's highest honor, even more so if she later sends her precious child off to die in battle.

Aristophanes' comedy *Lysistrata* from 411 B.C.E. is one statement about the kind of diplomatic and sexual power that women could wield even without having political rights. In this play, the women of Athens and Sparta, tired of losing their menfolk to endless warfare, stage a sex strike, hoping they can force their husbands into a peace treaty. Even in the late twentieth century, there are similar examples of women's communities refusing to have marital relations unless their husbands take action on local issues.[30]

Denied access to the male-mentor learning symposia which defined classical Greek culture, few Greek women wrote plays or philosophy, but two names are well known: Sappho and Hypatia. Sappho, who lived on the island of Lesbos in the seventh century B.C.E., ran a school for girls as well as wrote lyric poetry with woman-loving themes—hence, today Westerners still use the term *lesbian* to refer to a female homosexual. Some writers in the early twentieth century also used the term *sapphic*. Much of ancient Greek society was homoerotic without controversy, but after the introduction of Christianity, same-sex love was increasingly banned, and much of Sappho's poetry was burned; mere fragments remain from the larger range of her life's work. Hypatia, a brilliant Greek philosopher and mathematician, was a pagan as well as a lecturer at the time when Christian faith overtook Greece and Rome in the fifth century; she was in Egypt when, "In 415, a mob allegedly incited by the Christian clergy of the city fell upon her in the streets, tore her limb from limb, and burned her broken body."[31]

The progress from goddess-centric Crete, to legal limitations on mortal women in classical Athens, to Christianity's hostile attacks on learned women makes ancient Greece a perfect illustration of how women's status shifted from respect and power to second-class status. The example of bold women like Sappho and the Amazons, who seemed free to challenge or ignore men while cel-

---

[30] Suzan Fraser, "Turkish Women Using Feminine Wiles." *Santa Cruz Sentinel,* August 5, 2001.

[31] Harriman, p. 108.

ebrating a focus on women and girls, inspired women throughout increasingly repressive ages, and became symbolic of women's desire for independence and learning. During the 1970s, particularly in the United States, the concept of the Amazons as fierce outsiders who were victorious in their refusal to submit to male control enjoyed a large revival among lesbian artists. Rediscovering Sappho's poetry, some feminist activists reclaimed terms that were meant to insult women (*lesbian, battle-ax, Amazon, crone*), and began illustrating political art and jewelry with the *labrys* symbol—the Mycenaean double-bladed ax supposedly used by ancient Amazon warriors.

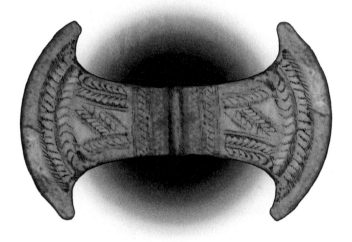

The Roman Empire

Ancient Rome posed many challenges for women, starting with the rape of the Sabine women by Roman men and ending with the consolidation of male religious power in the Roman Catholic Church (still centered in Rome's Vatican City today). The Latin language consolidated terms we still use to indicate male power and control: The *paterfamilias*, or oldest male head of a family, had complete authority over every other member of the household; *patrician* ruling males in the Senate upheld community standards (and gave us the common names Patrick and Patricia); society itself was *paternal*. Where ancient Greece had Aristotle regarding female bodies as weak and deformed, Rome had Pliny the Elder, who wrote that first-century volume called *Natural History* in which he described how a menstruating woman caused milk and wine to sour and vines to wither.

Yet Rome, too, had a goddess culture—Minerva, Diana, Juno; and a powerful, much-admired royal consort to men of state: Queen Cleopatra. The stately Roman matron might have enjoyed respect within the home, but like her Greek counterpart, she was limited politically. And Roman law allowed for female infanticide. Only men could initiate divorce; a husband had the legal authority to kill his wife for adultery or even for drinking; and a virgin who was raped was simply burned to death—as was a housewife who slept with one of her male servants. With Roman expansion into North Africa, Egypt's Cleopatra sought romantic alliances with Julius Caesar and Marc Antony. Dramatically, she joined Antony in suicide by allowing a deadly snake—an asp—to bite her breast. This is but one more of many roles that snakes play in depictions of goddesses, powerful women, and figures such as Eve. It was also seen as appropriate at that time in Rome for women to kill themselves rather than outlive their husbands: What was a woman without her man?

Although she was not Roman but an enemy of Rome, it's important to mention the dynamic British queen who fought the Romans' invasion of London in the early year of 60 C.E.–Queen Boudicca, a Briton of the first century, fiercely regarded.

Christianity

When Christianity came to Greece and Rome through the gospels of disciples such as Paul, women experienced both losses and gains. The spread of the new faith through the Mediterranean is easily seen in the geography of Bible chapters, many of which refer to Greek and Roman communities (Romans, Corinthians, Ephesians, and so on.) A new goddess appeared, for both women and men to worship, in the form of Mary, although many devout Christians today dispute whether Mary should be linked with goddess worship. Mary, as both Virgin and Blessed Mother, became revered as a person many women felt they could relate to: a poor girl with an unexplained pregnancy, forced to give birth in a humble barn; a grieving mother who lost a beloved son in a brutal act of public execution. Images of Madonna and child gave every mother cradling a newborn in her arms a saintly image celebrating maternal love: the ultimate female role. In their book *The Divine Feminine,* authors Andrew Harvey and Anne Baring comment, "In being named 'Mother of God' at the Council of Ephesus in 431, she was implicitly (though not doctrinally) recognized as the feminine counterpart of the Divine Father.... In her humanity, in her human suffering as the mother of Jesus, Mary brings the divine world closer to human experience, closer to human longing and human suffering." [32]

Jesus had encouraged women to learn and to prophesy (Acts 2:17), although, as Chapter One discusses, Paul advised against women teaching men, having authority over men, or speaking in church, and advised them to be subjects to their husbands. Still, devout female converts willingly allowed the Romans to throw them to the lions for the sake of Christian martyrdom (until 380, when Christianity became Rome's official state religion). Early Church Fathers, however, grew increasingly obsessed with the female body as the cause of all trouble, so that the old emphasis on women's powerful fertility seen in ancient goddess statues (and in Judaism) was replaced by the values of virginity, celibacy, and shame. After all, part of Mary's holiness was that she represented maternity without sexuality. Marriage was less honorable than virginity—the famous saying attributed to Saint Augustine, "It is better to marry than to burn." The early Church Fathers like Augustine, Jerome, and Tertullian were appalled by women's earthly carnality and urged them to resist the sex act inherent in marriage by dedicating themselves to chastity. By this time in history, even a traditionally devout wife lost virtue through the act of reproduction—seen in Christianity as a means of transmitting Original Sin to the next generation, and requiring baptism so that a newborn would not burn in hell. The doctrine emerging from these early centuries of male-interpreted Christianity overturned Judaism's first

[32] Andrew Harvey and Anne Baring, *The Divine Feminine.* Berkeley, CA: Conari Press, 1996; p. 106.

commandment: "Be fruitful and multiply." The new ideal for women was celibacy, and it became necessary to deny the body altogether to appear holy.[33] Many women eagerly took to extreme fasting, feeling that such physical self-denial would let them unite with the hunger and thirst suffered by Christ on the cross. Fasting also lessened the shame of women's sexual characteristics—natural curves wasted away, menstration stopped altogether.

Purging the body of all pleasures (sex, alcohol, married life) allowed the pious to transcend earthly temptations, and social historians like Joan Jacobs Brumberg and Rudolph Bell notice that this is the era when "holy anorexia" begins to appear in young women. Denying the body made one "good."

In fairness, the fourth century C.E. was also when the Church began to require abstinence for male priests. As convents and monasteries were built, common people speculated as to whether priests and nuns ever broke the rules with secret romances. More seriously, today's sex scandals created by wayward priests have led to new discussion about the challenges of lifelong chastity.

As you may have noticed, the Christianization of Europe had far-reaching effects on how we identify when events occurred historically. Europeans developed a religion-based time line, dividing life on earth into B.C. (Before Christ) and A.D. (Latin for *Anno Domini,* or Year of Our Lord). Women's history in the Western tradition is now written in these terms. But Jews, Muslims, and others may prefer to use C.E. and B.C.E. (Christian Era, Before the Christian Era) when referring to historical dates, and this is an acceptable scholarly choice. Historical time does not belong to one faith alone.

[33] See Rosemary Radford Ruether's essay "Misogyny and Virginal Feminism in the Fathers of the Church," in *Religion and Sexism*. New York: Simon & Schuster, 1974.

Most of us accept, with passive cooperation, the way scholarship defers to mainstream beliefs we may not participate in. What else do we accept without question?

This, too, is the story of women's history.

Radical Nuns

From the records of ancient Greece and Rome at the time Christianity arrived in Europe, we know it was customary for girls to be married off very young—typically to a much older man. Many, many girls died in childbirth, as they were likely to be pregnant at age 13 and 14; and Roman laws about the option of sacrificing any extra female babies struck terror in the hearts of young mothers. The poetry of Sappho speaks to Greek girls' fear of the wedding night, the loss of innocence to a stranger, in her poem *Bridesmaids' Carol II:* "Virginity O my Virginity! Where will you go when I lose you?", and the stark *Lament for a Maidenhead:* "... trampled by shepherds until only a purple stain remains on the ground."[34] How welcome the new idea of Christian celibacy must have seemed! Here was a respectable alternative to marriage and motherhood. Greece and Rome had one basically similar option already: vestal virgins, who were the only women permitted to live apart from men, tending goddess temples in a sacred sisterhood. Thus, the emerging model of convent life in a sisterhood of virginal Christian women was not really alien, and attracted many converts. Nuns were some of the first European women to be educated, and convents and monasteries allowed nuns to copy or illustrate Bibles centuries before the invention of the printing press. Nuns also served as teachers and visionaries whose words might be respected. Where other women were silenced, nuns had the authorization to speak. On the other hand, with the strict Christianization of Europe and other regions, traditional female shamans, faith healers, and leaders of spirit religions came under attack as pagans.

Not all convents were open to any pious girl. Most required a dowry for the lifelong financial care of a religious girl, and simi-

---

[34] Mary Barnard, *Sappho: A New Translation.* Berkeley: University of California Press, 1958.

lar to dowry marriage, a nun who took her vows became a "bride of Christ" and wore a wedding ring. While nuns, like the vestal virgins before them, were some of the only women permitted an alternative to married life and pregnancy, they were still subject to male control: the authority of priests. Powerful nuns like the famous twelfth-century Hildegard of Bingen might have mystical visions, compose sacred music, heal the sick, and write morality plays, but nuns expressing too many opinions faced charges of heresy. There was a fine line between being respectable and heretical. When we begin to see Christian women become known as writers, the content of their work had to satisfy the strict moral ideals of their world: Roswitha (or Hrosvitha), the first female playwright to emerge in the area of Germany in the tenth century, advocated virginity and the wickedness of sexuality in her plays.

Spinsters, Brewsters, and Wet Nurses

Ape Leader: An old maid: their punishment after death, for neglecting increase and multiply, will be, it is said, leading apes in hell. (*1811 Dictionary of Vulgar Tongue.*)

One of the tricks of history is that we tend to learn about famous people. Ordinary life isn't addressed as much as warfare, revolution, exploration and discovery, good kings and bad dictators. Ordinary *women* get even less press, for the very good reason that throughout history they were less likely than men to be educated, and so less likely to record their experiences. However, words and phrases can tell us a great deal about women's lives: Take a word like *spinster,* which even now means an unmarried woman. Spinning and textile work defined women's lives for much of history: Women were constantly spinning yarn, carding wool, and making clothing for their families. As peasants, women worked alongside men in the fields, brewed beer and ale, worked in taverns, shops, and as innkeepers, raised animals, and made cheese and soap. Despite the multiple skills women had in home production, they were not permitted to join craft guilds—for instance, weaving was considered a male profession. Gradually, there emerged a split between housework and what was considered "skilled," or waged, labor: "With the development of capitalism, work was increasingly defined as an activity for which one was paid, which meant that domestic tasks and childrearing were not considered work, unless they were done for wages."[35] Women's daily and seasonal work at home and in the fields, though exhausting, was part of a sexual division of labor that allowed men to be earners where women were caregivers—and, increasingly, laws such as the Netherlands' sixth-century Salic law favored sons and kept daughters from inheriting land. Women depended on men for protection and income. But there was one job a woman might do for pay that no man was qualified for: Lacking any other options, a woman who had recently given birth (and perhaps lost a child) could be a wet nurse to another woman's baby. In fact, this was a common job, and later on we see the important role of wet nurses in places as varied as Shakespeare (Juliet's nurse) and American slavery, where despite virulent racism and tight controls over contact between blacks and whites, slave-owning mistresses regularly handed over their children to slave women, who breast-fed them.[36]

In the medieval world we begin to see the establishment of male family names reflecting certain work identities (think of Baker, Taylor, Fisher, Farmer, Sawyer, Brewster, Webster, Cooper), but a woman lost her own family name when she married. The way that men could professionalize women's household work and elevate it

---

[35] Merry E. Wiesner, "Spinning Out Capital: Women's Work in Preindustrial Europe, 1350–1750," in Becoming Visible, p. 207.

[36] See Julia Cherry Spruill, *Women's Life and Work in the Southern Colonies.* New York: W.W. Norton, 1972 (first published by the University of North Carolina Press, 1938); pp. 55–57.

through guild membership can still be seen today: Around the world women do most of the cooking and sewing for their families, but today many fashion designers and famous chefs are men.

The Renaissance

We're all instructed to admire the great male artists from the fourteenth-century Renaissance and onward—Michelangelo, Leonardo da Vinci. What about the great women composers, sculptors, or artists who lived then? Were women simply not as creative as men? Too busy having kids? Or were they actively discouraged from painting and singing in an era when men were discovering their inner genius? These issues are explored in a wonderful book called *The Guerrilla Girls' Bedside Companion to the History of Western Art*. These "Guerrilla Girls" are a group of art activists dedicated to promoting work by female artists in museums and mainstream culture; their writings and lectures poke fun at sexism in the art world while raising serious points. Other historians agree that most women were unable to become great artists because they were married young, denied access to any sort of education, forbidden to be alone with a male mentor who might train them, molested by some men who did show up as mentors— and the subject matter of what "nice" women might draw, compose, or sculpt was strictly limited. Nude bodies? No. Women could not sing before men or rent an artist's studio without scandal. (The assumption being that keeping a private space meant you were having an affair. Even in the 1980s, single women might be turned away from renting a room or a house on the grounds that they might have premarital sex there; this issue became a raging court case in several U.S. states.)

Despite these conditions, women wrote and painted in every country, but those who succeeded often had to make the compromise of delaying marriage or finding an unusually supportive husband. Often their subject matter reflected their conditions as women, further sensationalizing what it meant to be a "woman artist." Christine de Pizan was married at fifteen, then widowed at twenty-five; she wrote to support herself through the fourteenth century, creating works that paid tribute to other learned and radical women, such as *The City of Ladies*. Artemesia Gentileschi became a phenomenal artist in the seventeenth century, only to be raped by a male artist named Agostino Tassi and then scorned during the rape trial which followed. Her famous painting shows the Biblical heroine Judith beheading the male Holofernes.

Famed British conductor Sir Thomas Beecham once sneered, "There are no women composers, there never have been, and possibly, there never will be," but from Hildegard of Bingen to Marianne Martines, women somehow managed to create and compose. By the thirteenth century almost no university in Europe allowed women to be educated; in her 1404 book *The City of Ladies,* Christine de Pizan pleaded for female education: "If it were customary to send daughters to school like sons, and if they were taught the natural sciences, they would learn as thoroughly and understand the subtleties of all the arts and sciences as well...." The thirteenth century is also when the Church formally banned contraception, and the average woman had many children, often dying in childbirth (or from miscarriages) well before the age of 21. If a woman wanted to postpone pregnancy, limit the size of her family, or just protect her maternal health in order to have more time to develop her art, where could she go for advice? Not to the Church, and not to a male physician, but to a midwife, of course.

Plagues, Crusades, Midwives, and Witchhunts

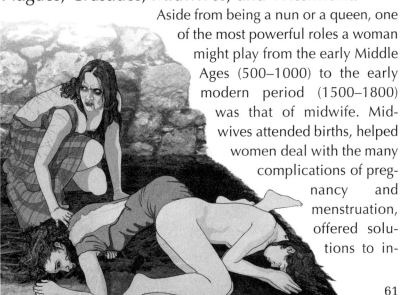

Aside from being a nun or a queen, one of the most powerful roles a woman might play from the early Middle Ages (500–1000) to the early modern period (1500–1800) was that of midwife. Midwives attended births, helped women deal with the many complications of pregnancy and menstruation, offered solutions to infertility and miscarriages, and were far better informed than most male physicians about birth control, abortion, and female sexual response.

The midwife was a combination of doctor and nurse. Unfortunately, women were banned from medical colleges as soon as the first universities opened and began formally training physicians. Not only were women denied the opportunity to gain medical degrees until the nineteenth century, but for almost five hundred years, few men in medical school studied the female body. It was the male body which set the anatomical standard, and the subject of obstetrics, gynecology, anything to do with female reproduction, remained secondary, keeping women's health a mystery.[37] Who tended women through their hours of labor, the tragedy of stillbirth, the challenges of menopause? Other women, in the time-honored role of midwife, granny, healer. Women soothed other women with treatments unknown to male doctors: including plant medicines, herbs, positions of the body, even furniture such as birthing stools. With so many young girls dying in premature labor or from misunderstood complications, the hour of birth was far too often the hour of maternal death. Records of women's household goods in the seventeenth century show that childbirth linen was a prized

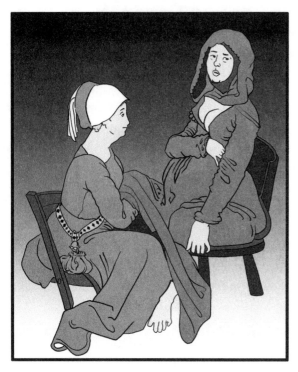

---

[37] Even as recently as the 1980s, the U.S. National Institutes of Health in Bethesda, Maryland, regularly released medical studies based on male subjects only, an issue tackled by local politician Connie Morella.

possession, brought out to pillow what might be a wife's final hours.[38]

Needless to say, childbirth "potions" and the apparently magical properties of midwives' brews, lent suspicion in Christian Europe that midwives were practicing witchcraft, or were even in cahoots with the Devil himself. A cultural term like *witch doctor* reflects the fear and disdain felt toward many independent female healers—although people in isolated communities relied on them.

Why did such hostility land on the shoulders of wise women who, in effect, performed a vital service to the female population? It seems that no matter where we look in women's history, reproductive powers are the most controversial aspects of womanhood. Where midwives sought to heal the intimate problems of miscarriage, infertility, postpartum depression (a serious condition barely understood even now), birth defects, and breastfeeding complications, they could also be blamed for these problems, even charged with deliberately cursing a marriage or causing an infant to be stillborn. Living in ignorance of sexually transmitted diseases and reproductive health, peasant communities both relied on and reacted to the often elderly women who held the keys to rudimentary birth control and abortion. Three main reasons that midwives were persecuted: They eased the pain of birth, and of course painful labor is God's "curse" to Eve and all women. They practiced medicine without formal education, allowing educated men to look down on them and less-educated people to fear the source of midwives' knowledge. And they were often older women without husbands, earning a living the only way they knew, but seemingly not subject to male authority of any kind. After the Black Plague decimated more males than females in Europe in the fourteenth and fifteenth centuries, leaving a surplus of women in the population, there were many unmarried, aging women who needed a means of supporting themselves.

The *witch burnings* followed patterns set in motion by the Catholic Church (and, later, the Protestant Reformation, as we

---

[38] See Julia Cherry Spruill, *Women's Life and Work in the Southern Colonies.*

know from Colonial America's Salem witch trials). For Christianity to be centralized as a way of life, folkways and practices associated with "pagan" beliefs had to be stamped out—brutally and lethally, on countless instances. Soon after the printing press was invented, a widely circulated manual called the *Malleus Malificarum* ("The Hammer of Witches") was commissioned by Pope Innocent VII in 1484. It began to be used by priests to collect confessions by women (and men) charged with witchcraft, and played a critical role in the trials of the Inquisition through the fifteenth, sixteenth, and seventeenth centuries. Accused women were tortured, their confessions of little honest worth but serving to set up huge spectacles of public burning. The National Film Board of Canada's excellent documentary *The Burning Times* describes how witch burnings silenced women's power; one historian interviewed in the film suggests, "We did have a women's holocaust; it may have been as many as nine million." Today, women and girls are still jailed for alleged witchcraft in Central and Western Africa; in 2004 Scotland offered a pardon for 3,500 women, children, *and cats* executed by the Baron Courts in the sixteenth and seventeenth centuries.

Women were also burned at the stake for other aspects of heresy. Even celebrated women who had led extraordinarily valiant lives were not spared; the best-known example is Jeanne D'Arc (Joan of Arc). With cropped hair, and dressed as a male warrior, young Joan led the French army to victory over the English at Orleans in 1429. But despite her celebrated and heroic role, when captured the following year, Joan was thrown in prison and charged with violating the Biblical prohibition against wearing clothing of the opposite sex. She was burned at the stake in 1431 for dressing as a man, becoming one of history's most famous martyrs. Interestingly, the ban against cross-dressing was eventually made law in the United States. Women and men were arrested for daring to dress in the wrong garb, if not actually burned alive. In Louisiana, Mardi Gras became one day of the year when citizens could legally cross-dress without being harassed by police. American playwright Carolyn Gage's excellent one-woman script, *The Second Coming of Joan of Arc*, offers a new way to reexamine the life of this misunderstood heroine.[39]

Women as Bloodthirsty Queens and Pirates

Many Americans are fascinated by the lineage of queens around the world; in the United States a woman running for President still attracts controversy. Queens might wield power, but for most of history they were likely to inherit the throne when lineage passed through key ruling families; as with Egyptian Pharaohs, queens sometimes ruled when kings (or other male heirs to the throne) were physically or mentally ill. Even in elite families, women were at the mercy of husbands; for centuries, both local and religious laws allowed husbands to beat their wives—known as "moderate correction" in England (and endorsed by at least some doctors as late as 1964 in the United States).[40] The twelfth-century Eleanor of Aquitane, at one point queen of France *and* England, wore armor and fought in the Crusades, but later married England's Duke of Normandy (King Henry II), who put her under house arrest for 15 years and confiscated her valuable, inherited lands.

When Martin Luther began the Protestant Reformation in 1517,

---

[39] Carolyn Gage, *The Second Coming of Joan of Arc*. Santa Cruz, CA: HerBooks, 1994.

[40] Reported by Stephanie Coontz, "Gay Marriage Isn't Revolutionary," *Washington Post* 2011.

several important new reforms affected women directly. Luther held that marriage was no longer a sacrament, making divorce possible again; and he encouraged literacy for women as well as men, so that individuals might take responsibility for their own salvation through Bible study. On the other hand, the Reformation's backlash against the Church also had devastating consequences for women, too: Convents were attacked and closed. Celibacy gradually ended as a religious ideal for Protestant Christians; this meant that scholarly, unmarried Catholic nuns were ridiculed, rather than respected. As neighbor turned against neighbor in the proliferation of new religious sects, witch burnings did not stop; they began to target Protestant women who dared to preach, like Anne Hutchinson, who was put on trial and killed in Salem, Massachusetts in 1636.

In their zeal to profess Christian belief, or just to protect themselves from being accused, women as well as men might cross the line from piety to acting as persecutor. A climate of fear and witch-hunting gave everyday women the means to settle old scores of jealousy or dislike by accusing a neighbor of heresy, and during the high Middle Ages we find various queens, in particular, abusing their powers as ruling monarchs. In Catholic Spain, Queen Isabella's piety extended to ordering the Inquisition for accused nonbelievers, as well as the expulsion of Jews and Muslims from her lands. In England, after the Protestant Reformation, Mary Tudor ("Bloody Mary") persecuted new Protestants to restore Catholicism in the land, while Elizabeth I restored Anglican power but placed Mary, Queen of Scots, under house arrest and finally had her executed. The famous queen of *Alice in Wonderland* who shouts "Off with their heads!" hearkens back to these bloodthirsty monarchs. One male author, John Knox, was so opposed to the rule of queens that, in 1558, he wrote a book with the interesting title: *First Blast of the Trumpet Against the Regiment of Monstrous Women.*

That some queens supplied the funds for the Age of Exploration and, by extension, underwrote the slave trade, is another complicated story. But as men sought to discover and conquer new lands, greed as well as a desire for excitement spurred some women to disguise themselves as capable boy sailors. A few were fleeing forced marriages; others needed work; and yes, some were attracted to a lifestyle of crime and plunder. But considering the restrictive roles for most women in the sixteenth century, who wouldn't want to be a pirate? Grace O'Malley, or Granuaile, was known as Western Ireland's "Pirate Queen," so important a figure that in 1593, at age 63, she actually met with Queen Elizabeth I. Her wild life was turned into a successful Broadway musical in 2006. Two pirates who dressed and passed as men are Mary Read and Anne Bonny, who sailed with John Rackham ("Calico Jack"), raiding Jamaica and the Bahamas around 1720.

Slavery and Colonization

The onset of the *slave trade* opened a chapter of history that both Africa and the West have yet to recover from. Slavery as an institution of course dates back far earlier than the racially specific system established in the eighteenth and nineteenth century United States; it was part of life in the Middle East, ancient Greece and Rome, Islamic trade, within many African tribes, and its practices are referenced throughout the Bible and Koran. But beyond the routine exchange and sale of captives seized in war, the European trade in human life emerged in the 1500s with Spanish and Portuguese "slavers," and grew to include raids on specific tribes such as the Ibo of Nigeria. Women and girls were shackled together in *coffles,* marched to the sea, held in stockades, and then shipped to Spanish, Portuguese, Dutch, British, and French colonies in the New World (the Americas and the Caribbean) in what we call the *Middle Passage* of terrifying confinement onboard; at least one in ten died during the six to eight-week voyage. Ten million slaves were brought to the New World. In the West Indies, South America, and then later the colonies of Virginia, Georgia, and the Carolinas, slave women were forced into exhausting agricultural labor in sugarcane and cotton fields, where they also were vulnerable to rape and forced breeding by owners. Little to no regard was shown for their bodies or sensibilities as women; females were branded under the breast, sold at auction based on apparent physical strength and fertility, and whipped for any act of rebellion.

The profitability of slaves began to replace the old system of importing young women as *indentured servants*—girls who might be badly treated as housemaids but who generally earned their freedom after seven years. (Indentured servants were once sold like slaves, too: Benjamin Franklin's indentured grandmother married the man who bought her.) The first female African captives arrived in the colonies of North America around 1619; by the time of the American Revolution, slaves were two-thirds of the population of South Carolina and half the population of Virginia, lacking any legal protection or recognized legal standing for their own children and marriages.

English, Irish, and Scots women who followed their communities of conscience to the new colonies of Massachusetts, Pennsylvania, or Rhode Island included Puritans and Quakers, wives of planters and landowning ministers, and indentured servants hoping to leave behind the dead-end London of poorhouses or life below stairs in England's rigid class system. In the New World, European migrants encountered Native American women from countless tribes—some with deeply entrenched practices of matriarchy and female governance. White settlers' desire to Christianize indigenous groups (when Indians were not slaughtered outright) defined the relationship between white and Native women; while sometimes mutually supportive, interactions were more often patronizing, adversarial, even genocidal. By the time of the American Revolution, both colonists and British troops enlisted the help of Indian women as spies and scouts, promising autonomy and land rights to those who aided their cause. Under Colonial law, white women had almost as few political rights as women of color, especially as indentured servants; and while some white male colonists intermarried with Native women or had forcible sex with their female slaves, white women could be flogged, pilloried, or hanged for giving birth to an illegitimate or mixed-race baby.[41] (The story of *The Scarlet Letter,* with its descriptions of the outlook on female adultery, is familiar to many.) And those who migrated for religious freedom could only go so far in the new land, as Anne Hutchinson and others soon learned.

Workhouses and Factories of the Industrial Revolution

During the seventeenth century, women across Europe found their traditional work of home production being redefined by new factories in the growing wage economy. What was once handmade at home—clothing, soap, candles, liquor, shoes, bedding, and other household goods—could now be mass-produced by new

methods of industry, mainly textile looms in airless factories and workhouses, where girls and women were paid far less than men for the same work and subject to sexual harassment as well. As England's Enclosure Acts withdrew common grazing lands from peasant farmers and herders, men and women who knew no other living than agricultural labor migrated to distant cities for waged work, easy prey for unscrupulous employers in the early factory decades. Often abandoned by husbands, left destitute, women and children dependent on

[41] Julia Cherry Spruill, *Women's Life and Work in the Southern Colonies;* pp. 55–57, 334–335. New York: W.W. Norton, 1972; first published by University of North Carolina Press, 1938.

the meager charity of the Poor Laws ended up in the system of workhouses and orphanages, grimly portrayed by Charles Dickens and other authors. Young girls who labored "below stairs" as servants in the homes of the wealthy might gain greater access to food, but, like household slaves in the colonies, were also more likely to be seduced or raped by masters and their sons. Turned out into the snow without references, sometimes impregnated by a young man of the household, these disgraced servant girls were some of the desperate emigrants who sought a new life in America. (Not all who came over were Puritans.)

The Enlightenment, Revolution, and Women's Changing Roles

By the eighteenth century, a Europe weary of witch trials and repression saw prominent intellectuals emerge with rational approaches to human rights. But these "great minds" of the modern age—male philosophers who expressed profoundly important ideas about individual human liberty and free thought—were usually repressive (or silent) on the topic of expanding women's rights. Thomas Locke supported women's subordination as natural. Jean-Jacques Rousseau proposed a more educated society, but believed it wasn't necessary to educate girls beyond what they should know in order to make men happy.[42] This view infuriated English writer Mary Wollstonecraft, who knew from personal experience (her own dysfunctional mother, and earning her own living as a governess) that an educated and rational mother was better equipped to support her own children—especially when fathers and husbands failed as

"A HYENA IN PETTICOATS"

[42] Gerda Lerner, *The Creation of Feminist Consciousness*, 211.

providers. Wollstonecraft's groundbreaking volume *A Vindication of the Rights of Woman* (1792) ushered in an era of new debate over female learning and liberty in the West. Although she was vilified—famously referred to as a "hyena in petticoats" by one sour male critic—Wollstonecraft was one of the first of many feminist writers to suggest that a marriage of equals might be possible, even desirable. She also dared to link the right to equal education with human progression overall, granting that women offered more to civilization than just marital servitude: "Till women are more rationally educated, the progress of human virtue and improvement in knowledge must receive continual checks ... if it be granted that woman was not created merely to gratify the appetite of man, or to be the upper servant, who provides his meals and takes carte of his linen."[43]

Wollstonecraft, along with advocates for women's education in the newly emerging United States, put Enlightenment spin on a fairly traditional idea: that children benefit from wise and well-prepared mothers, not foolish ones. Across cultures and borders, the argument for *educated motherhood* expanded schooling for girls in general. Convent schooling continued for girls who could afford it, mostly as a bulwark against the expansion of Protestant thought, but the beginning of public education included girls as well as boys (though not at all levels or in all countries). And gradually, such late eighteenth-century ideals of rational motherhood helped create the fusion of domestic skills and scholarship we still call "home economics," a subject popularized later on by earnest reformers like Catharine Beecher. Still, as historian Linda Kerber noted, "We are left with an intellectual gap. The great treatises of the Enlightenment, which criticized and helped to change attitudes toward the state, offered no guidance to women analyzing their relationship to liberty or civic virtue.... For Locke, Montesquieu, Rousseau and Kames, women existed only as mothers and wives."[44]

---

[43] Mary Wollstonecraft, *A Vindication of the Rights of Woman.* In *The Feminist Papers,* ed. Alice Rossi; Columbia University Press, 1973; p. 54.

[44] Linda Kerber, *Women of the Republic.* New York: W.W. Norton, 1986; p. 27.

As women were drawn to the Enlightenment ideals of their time, they participated in both the French and American revolutions—although these uprisings also pitted woman against woman where political and class interests trumped gender. The thousands of Frenchwomen who took part in the Bread Riots, marching from Paris to the Palace at Versailles in 1789, were hardly on the same page as their nemesis, the elite queen Marie Antoinette. (She's supposed to have replied "Let them eat cake" when told that the poor mothers had no bread, but this is just rumor—it's a line suggested by Rousseau decades earlier.)

In the American colonies, women whose husbands were loyal to England's King George were expected to support both husband and king, rather than joining with other women in Daughters of Liberty actions against the crown. Native American women like Nancy Ward (Cherokee) and Mollie Brandt (Iroquois) were recruited for opposing sides; the British offered freedom to loyal slaves willing to fight the colonists, but later sold most back to the West Indies. Sisterhood vanished within race, rank, and rebellion.

Wartime and revolution opened up opportunities as it politicized women, but not without risk. Lacking a marriage dowry, barely earning her bread as a servant, Deborah Sampson passed as a young male soldier named Robert Shurtleff in order to fight (and to get a man's pay). However, historian Carol Berkin reminds us that other women caught passing as male might be lashed and marched out of army camps while the band played a tune called the "Whore's March." And whether sons and husbands fought with British troops or for General George Washington, the women left behind found that taking over men's work was "a nightmare, not liberation," as it doubled their usual workload.[45] (Slave women already assigned masculine work without care for their maternity or strength had long known that being forced into men's jobs did not equal feminist progress.) The American Revolution, beginning with the tea boycott, also hardened women's lives by asking them to give up all imported (English) goods: food, clothing, and comforts

[45] Carol Berkin, "It Was I Who Did It: Women in the American Revolution," presented at the AP College Board U.S. History Reading in Louisville, KY, June 7, 2008.

such as tea. This role of housewife as a political *consumer* would emerge in every subsequent war and play a role in the development of advertising.

"...I defire you would Remember the Ladief...Do not put fuch unlimited power into the handf of Hufbandf."

Hoping to see new rights for women written into the American Constitution, Abigail Adams petitioned her husband John: "In the new Code of Laws which I suppose it will be necessary for you to make I desire you would Remember the Ladies, and be more generous and favorable to them than your ancestors. Do not put such unlimited power into the hands of Husbands."[46] But those women who gave their all for liberty in the French and American revolutions would grow sorely disappointed in the aftermath of the war

[46] Abigail Adams to John Adams, March 31, 1776. In Rossi, ed., *The Feminist Papers;* p. 10.

years; France's Napoleonic Code of 1804 forbade women from signing contracts or carrying out financial transactions in their own names. In the new America of democracy and rule by the people, most of the old Colonial laws limiting women's rights remained: White women, slaves of both sexes, and men and women from indigenous tribes would find the Constitution guaranteed them neither liberty nor citizenship. Women could still not testify in court, sue, sign contracts, control their own property after marriage, or vote. For black women of differing circumstances, race rather than gender determined alliances with men: as indicated in Chapter One, founding father Thomas Jefferson became romantically linked with his slave mistress Sally Hemmings, fathering their many descendents. And the brilliant young slave Phillis Wheatley, the first African-American woman to publish her writing, won praise from George Washington, but later had to prove in court that, as an African slave, she was indeed literate enough to be the author of her own work. Although her master had encouraged her scholarship and promoted her poetry, he also did not grant her freedom until his own death; by then Phillis (named for the very slave ship which brought her from Africa) was almost 25. Her life is an additional reminder that throughout early America, slave ownership was not limited to the Southern colonies. She had been sold at age nine in Boston's slave market.

From Republican Motherhood to Abolition and the Birth of First-Wave Feminism

If women lacked rights in post-Revolutionary America, they were nonetheless expected to find duty and empowerment as mothers of citizen sons. Dating back to ancient Greece and Rome, this concept reappeared as *Republican Motherhood* in the early nineteenth century, when women in the young United States were encouraged to shape the nation's future by instilling moral values at home. To the surprise of many statesmen, female reformers instead used their assigned maternal roles to argue for social change. The ideal of sacred motherhood gave women a platform for demanding better treatment of mothers—and that meant educated motherhood, as well as ending slavery, which notoriously separated mother from babe right at public auction.

Nineteenth-century ideals of rational motherhood helped create a new breed of housewife-activist, as well as introducing a new field called "home economics." Reformers including Catharine Beecher and Lydia Child elevated housewifely arts to a new level of training and management, making it more likely and appropriate for women to study scientific inventions, health, and accounting. But these white home economists also linked female dignity in the domestic sphere with demands to end slavery, joining with other abolitionists. Known for publishing *The Frugal Housewife* in 1832, Lydia Child was also busy hiding runaway slave mothers in her home.

As a religious movement called the Second Great Awakening swept from upstate New York to the American frontier, its leaders urged Christian women to speak out for the sort of *reforms* critical to building a moral society. However, pious mothers found they were reprimanded when they wrote of slavery's evils, and naming the national sin of sexual abuse proved especially controversial, as it revealed the hypocrisy of powerful men who claimed to "protect" women. Angelina Grimke's 1836 *Appeal to the Christian Women of the South* called on white women to practice civil disobedience by helping runaway slave mothers (and teach them to read and write). Her writings acknowledged that while women were not able to vote for social change, they could still collectively break the law. As historian Alice Rossi shows in *The Feminist Papers,* Grimke outraged many white men, including a Massachusetts church association which issued a complaint toward any woman who "assumes the place and tone of a man as a public reformer.... We especially deplore the intimate acquaintance and promiscuous conversation of females with regard to things which ought not to be named."[47] How could the sexual abuse of slave women end as a permitted practice when no one was supposed to tell the truth about it?[48]

Sojourner Truth, born a slave and given the name Isabella Baumfree by her Dutch owners, gained freedom and then fame for her powerful "Ain't I a Woman?" speech, delivered at the Ohio Women's Convention in 1851. Here she challenged her audience of male and female reformers to examine the ways nineteenth-century chivalry towards women never included *black* women. Such words were particularly important, because some white feminists argued for suffrage by comparing their own limited rights to enslavement, ignoring enormous differences in the treatment and opportunities of white and black women. Although all women were denied political rights, social and legal privileges were still accorded to black and white women unequally.

> That man over there says that women need to be helped into carriages, and lifted over ditches, and to have the best place everywhere. Nobody ever helps me into carriages, or over mud-puddles, or gives me any best place! And ain't I a woman? Look at me! Look at my arm! I have ploughed, and planted, and gathered into barns, and no man could head me! And ain't I a woman? I could work as much and eat as much as a man—when I could get it—and bear the lash as well! And ain't I a woman? I have borne thirteen children, and seen most all sold off into slavery, and when I cried out with my mother's grief, none but Jesus heard me! And ain't I a woman?

---

[47] From a Pastoral Letter, 'The General Association of Massachusetts (Orthodox) to the Churches Under Their Care," 1837. In Alice Rossi, *The Feminist Papers,* pp. 305–306.

[48] The ways slave women practiced resistance is another story. See Kara Walker's controversial silhouettes of this history, recently exhibited at the Whitney Museum of American Art.

Most historians see the *first wave of feminism* in the United States beginning with abolitionist activism. Lucretia Mott and Elizabeth Cady Stanton traveled to the World Antislavery Convention in London, 1840, only to find that as women they were barred from entry. Later, Stanton and four Quaker women organized the first women's rights convention in Seneca Falls, New York. (The idea emerged during a party Jane Hunt threw for Lucretia Mott on July 9, 1848. Never underestimate the power of women's dinner parties.)

For the women's rights convention, the women decided to draft a Declaration of Sentiments modeled on Thomas Jefferson's ideals in the Declaration of Independence. In her book *Reminiscences,* finished in 1897, Stanton would recall "Night after night, by an old-fashioned fireplace, we plotted and planned the coming agitation." At the conference, attended by male as well as female supporters, first-wave feminism burst into action with a reading of democracy's ongoing outrages against women. From this beginning, nineteenth-century activists took up multiple causes: abolition, suffrage (the vote), education, work wages, married women's property rights, access to medical and law school, and much more. Many women campaigned against alcohol, which they saw as a key factor in male domestic abuse of women and children, and some, like Stanton, began writing feminist criticism of religion: in her *Woman's Bible,* she argued that women would never be emancipated as long as they accepted men's interpretations of their place in society.

Elizabeth Cady Stanton and Susan B. Anthony would devote their own lives to what was ultimately an eighty-year campaign for women to be full, voting citizens: Stanton as the writer, drafting speeches at home, and the unmarried Anthony as the campaigner and speaker on the road. When the United States Senate first introduced a women's suffrage amendment on January 10, 1878, it was called the Susan B. Anthony Amendment.

Civil War Heroines and Nurses

Slavery was not fully abolished until the Thirteenth Amendment in 1865. For another generation after the Seneca Falls convention, American women along the Underground Railroad route to Northern freedom hid runaway slaves in their homes and barns. Many of the runaways were mothers and children terrified of separation, sale, and sexual abuse; and escaped slaves like Harriet Tubman returned over and over at great risk to lead other families to freedom.

Harriet Tubman
1822-1913

Barbara Wertheimer describes Tubman's multiple leadership roles: "Her work continued throughout the Civil War as a scout, spy, and nurse. At the Combahee River she led a band of three hundred black soldiers on a raid to free eight hundred slaves—the only woman in American history ever to have led troops in battle. She nursed ex-slaves and wounded black soldiers in hospitals, using her knowledge of herbs to save many seriously ill with dysentery."[49]

White women who participated in abolitionist actions campaigned and organized, gaining skills in fund-raising and public speaking; some, like Harriet Beecher Stowe, the author of *Uncle Tom's Cabin*, produced books with an antislavery message. Still lacking the vote, white women in the U.S. gained agency through the Married Women's Property Acts of 1848 and 1860, which allowed them to control their own land and wages, sue in court, and share custody in the instance of divorce.

While the debate over slave mothers, women's education, and

---

[49] Barbara Mayer Wertheimer, *We Were There!* New York: Pantheon, 1977; p. 117. In the 1970s, an important political statement emerged from a group of black women calling themselves the Combahee River Collective, a reference to Tubman's raid.

women's suffrage raged, the mid-nineteenth century saw an increase in medical roles for women, as more and more men lost lives in the Crimean War and the Civil War in the United States. In 1849, Elizabeth Blackwell became the first American woman to receive a medical degree, graduating from Geneva Medical College in upstate New York—where her male classmates had first voted to admit her as a joke. Nursing gained new prominence during the years of bloodshed between North and South. It had long been accepted for some women to accompany their husbands in wartime as "camp followers" to personally care for them, yet it was still considered immodest for a woman to assist other men wounded in battle—an attitude changed by Florence Nightingale's service on the battlefields of the Crimean War. The Civil War in the U.S. required the caregiving skills of all women willing to become nurses and hospital workers, allowing spectacular figures to emerge in leadership roles unthinkable before wartime. Dorothea Dix became Superintendent of Army Nurses (who were required to be over thirty and "plain"), while Clara Barton used her wartime medical experience to found the Red Cross in 1882.[50] Dr. Mary Edwards Walker was commissioned as a first lieutenant and assistant surgeon, the highest rank held by a woman in the Civil War; and Sally Louisa Tompkins, known as "Captain Sally," was made the only female officer in the Confederate Army for her organization of a nursing hospital in Richmond. Of the 1,333 patients she treated there, only 73 died.

Throughout the Civil War, the participation of women was certainly not limited to traditional caregiving roles. Some, like Belle Boyd and "Wild Rose" O'Neale, acted as spies for the Confederacy, organizing other women and girls; others smuggled goods right under their hoop skirts—or passed as men to fight, to earn money, or to go West without harassment. Women also wrote of their wartime experiences: Mary Chesnut's famous diary revealed a Southern white woman's ambivalence toward the slave system, while Susan King Taylor, a nurse with the 33rd U.S. Colored Troops, published *Reminiscences of My Life in Camp*. After the

[50] Barbara Wertheimer, pp. 134–135.

Susan King-Taylor 1848-1912

war, women continued to defy convention in new ways: in 1866 Cathay Williams became the first black woman to enlist in the U.S. Army, serving with the 38th U.S. Infantry under the name William Cathay, and possibly never discovered to be female. But not all female "firsts" in the Civil War era stemmed from progress. In 1865, Mary Surratt became the first woman executed by the U.S. government, hanged for her much-debated role in the assassination of Abraham Lincoln. As a female, who was also menstruating at the time of her imprisonment before trial, she was treated differently than the male co-conspirators and permitted a rocking chair, bonnet, and fan.

Even as women showed skill in saving lives, and carried on earning their own living as widows after the brutal war years, the women's movement in the United States struggled to advance. Enormous divisions between Northern and Southern, black and white women precluded any unified feminism, especially after the Fifteenth Amendment in 1870 gave the right to vote to freed black males. This outraged some white suffragists, whose propaganda became more of a racist rationale for giving white women political power. And, as women entered more of public society as speakers, organizers, teachers, and wage workers, information on their own health and potential remained distorted by male medical authorities. In the second half of the nineteenth century, concerns about women overexerting themselves with work, study, or athletic training continued earlier beliefs such as Aristotle's "wandering womb" theory, and cautions against female hysteria dominated medical literature portraying women as "diseased."

Supposedly ruled by their ovaries, believed to have limited energy in their bodies, women were warned to avoid excitement or overwork, and male doctors (the American Medical Association had no female members until 1915) used leeches to treat "female complaints" like hysteria. Some prescribed clitoridectomies to control women who masturbated or had too hearty an interest in sex; the most enthusiastic was Dr. Isaac Baker Brown, who was elected president of London's Medical Society in 1865.[51] One Harvard Medical School professor, Dr. Edward Hammond Clark, threatened that higher education would make women insane. In his 1873 book *Sex in Education: Or, A Fair Chance for Girls,* he argued that "Identical education of the two sexes is a crime before God and humanity."[52]

Amelia Bloomer was one nineteenth-century reformer who sensibly argued that if women were often sick, dress was a contributing factor. Corsets and "stays" that laced women's ample figures into breathless constraint played tragic roles in a high incidence of maternal death, but the boyish loose trousers she promoted (later called *bloomers*), although popularized by the actress Fanny Kemble, shocked a population unaccustomed to seeing women in pants. Lack of clean water, indoor plumbing, toilet paper, refrigeration, good walking shoes, and other comforts we take for granted today all contributed to lower life expectancies and illness in wealthy as well as impoverished women (and men, too). Women used washable rags as discreetly as possible for

[51] See Peter Feibleman, "Natural Causes," in *DoubleTake,* v. 7, 1997; pp. 41–46.

[52] See Helga Harriman, p. 270.

their menstrual periods, kept dried corncobs or old sheets of newspapers handy in the outhouse, and coped as best they could with pregnancy under conditions that ranged from slavery to frontier life to factory labor. (Most American women took off corsets for good during World War I, when war work demanded an adjustment of sensible clothing; my great-aunt Sybil recalled her own relief when corsets were replaced by what she referred to as "two-way stretchers"—meaning brassieres.)

Teachers, Missionaries, and Women's Colleges

Where the theory of "female delicacy" kept women from higher education, they might pursue a passion for books and adventure by working as remotely placed schoolteachers or Christian missionaries. In the West, such roles—teacher, librarian, Sunday School missionary—reinforced images of women as prim, unmarried, sexless, pious, and lonely. Theirs was a "civilizing" influence over the so-called Wild West, a stereotype which did open up certain opportunities: America's first female policewoman, Lola Baldwin, was hired by the police department of Portland, Oregon, in 1908.

An individual woman might relish her calling, but popular culture, while finding single women useful for "good works" and office organizing, portrayed these figures as pitiful old maids. In the

United States and Canada, thousands of women went West as teachers and church workers, with mixed results: both white and African-American missionaries took part in the great displacement of indigenous native culture, beliefs, and practices. As "schoolmarms," who enjoyed the right to vote in school-board elections (school suffrage), female teachers who went West helped Wyoming become the first state to grant the vote to women in the nineteenth century. (This didn't mean that teachers' lives weren't burdened with exhausting codes of gender etiquette: a 1915 *Teacher's Magazine* "Rules of Conduct for Teachers" shows that female teachers could not marry, smoke, dress in bright colors, travel without permission, "keep company with men," etc.)

The fight for a university education was another story. By the late nineteenth century, colleges ranging from Oberlin (which admitted women in 1837) to the elite Seven Sisters colleges (Barnard, Bryn Mawr, Mount Holyoke, Radcliffe, Smith, Vassar, and Wellesley) flaunted the fears of Dr. Edward Clark by offering an advanced curriculum for women. However, as 60 percent of Smith graduates in 1884 did not marry, some critics believed that medical fears of scholarly sterility must be true. In fact, both the teaching and nursing professions required that women remain unmarried. Other graduates of women's colleges pooled their small incomes and lived together in what were called "Boston marriages," setting up households that no doubt included committed lesbian partnerships. Lillian Faderman's study *To Believe in Women* shows the extent to which lesbian scholars devoted their lives to furthering academic opportunities for other women; and Lynn Peril's humorous *College Girls* is a volume exploring the often ridiculous rules which limited the female "coed" once public and private colleges opened to her. In Europe, women from as far away as Russia journeyed to Switzerland once the University of Zurich opened to women in 1864; women could not earn actual degrees at colleges in Russia, or from Cambridge or Oxford, until the First World War.

For black women, the struggle for advanced education was inseparable from the endless fight against racism. Continuing the efforts of 1830s advocate Maria Stewart, black women like Nannie Burroughs established colleges, training schools, religious seminaries, and suffrage organizations; and in 1881 Spelman College opened for young black women in Atlanta, Georgia. Writing *A Voice From the South* in 1892, black suffragist Anna Julia Cooper sought to convince white women (as well as white men) of the moral and intellectual potential of black women as full, voting citizens. Such advocacy was undermined at every turn by the policies of the late nineteenth century, which kept women of color separate and unequal.

Population Control and Separation of the Races

The end of the nineteenth century saw global power shifts that were particularly insulting for women. Pope Leo XIII's 1891 letter *Quod Apostolici Muneris De Rerum Novarum* called the subjection of women essential to the Christian family. All women were excluded from the newly convened Olympic games of 1896. As the United States expanded into an empire, the great Queen Lili'uokalani was forced off the Hawaiian throne and placed under house arrest in her own Iolani Palace when American landowners, backed

Queen Lili'uokalani (1838-1917.)
Last Queen of Hawai'i.

by the U.S. Navy, staged action to make Hawaii into an American territory controlled by white business interests. Those unfamiliar with Queen Lil's role in defending indigenous rule—and her matriarchal Hawaiian ancestors—may recognize the popular ballad she composed, *Aloha Oe,* or "Farewell to Thee."[53]

---

[53] For two very different approaches to Hawaiian history, read Sarah Vowell's *Unfamiliar Fishes,* Riverhead Books, 2011, and Kiana Davenport's *Shark Dialogues,* Penguin, 1995.

Col. John Milton Chivington (1821-1894)
Officer. Preacher. Mass murderer.

Obsession with racial difference and classification in law, science, medicine, sports, and rule characterized the 1890s. In some instances laws against "inferior" groups were so punitive that populations shrank altogether from the genocidal policies of Indian wars, forced removal, landlessness, alcoholism, and European-introduced diseases (including syphilis). By 1892, the Native American population had decreased from almost two million to 300,000. Women and children were not spared in attacks meant to contain Native power; one commander, Colonel John Milton Chivington, justified his slaughter of Cheyenne and Arapaho women and children at the Sand Creek Massacre of 1864 with the explanation: "Nits make lice." The Dawes Act (1887) restructured surviving tribal communities into the reservation system—naming male heads of families as land owners, disenfranchising female elders. Indians did not receive American citizenship until 1924 (Utah did not allow Indians to vote until 1956), and Asian immigrants were unable to become naturalized U.S. citizens until 1943.

Many of these regulations, first passed in the 1870s, 80s, and 90s, resulted from the expansion of empire—a pattern repeated in the colonial race policies the British, French, Belgian, and Dutch governments introduced in India, Australia, New Zealand, the Caribbean, Siam, sub-Saharan Africa, and many more nations. For the United States, "empire" began with victory in the Spanish-American War, resulting in control over such island nations as Guam, Puerto Rico, the Philippines, and part of Cuba. Most colonial laws restricted the education and political power of nonwhite women in the same era when white women made gains toward fuller citizenship. Although colonial controls turned local women into subjects, occupation also reinforced cultural identities women could rally around as activists and agents of resistance, often in solidarity with men of their own communities.

Women and men of color were frequently exhibited as public spectacles as white scientists grew more interested in classifying racial difference. The most famous woman to be "displayed" for her racial body type was Sarah Baartje, brought to London as early as 1810 from South Africa and exhibited as the *Hottentot Venus*. After she died, her skeleton was retained and placed on exhibit in Paris (only recently have her bones been returned to South Africa). By the late nineteenth century, it was common for traveling sideshows to exhibit African or Asian males and females as human curiosities (alongside human "freaks" with grotesque physical differences). Such practices were meant to showcase other world peoples as primitive compared to the Caucasian West. Anthropologists' use of museums to exhibit skeletons, and photographs of bare-breasted women from indigenous tribes, further reinforced Western beliefs that only so-called "savages" dressed in clothing that revealed their limbs; missionaries introduced heavy, full-length dresses to the women of Hawaii, Polynesia, and Africa.

The fear of too many brown people soon led to backlash against white *birth control*. Contraception had been largely a private matter in the U.S. for over one hundred years; although it's important to note that Puritan settlers had been some of the most strident opponents to birth control: "As the woman bred and bore children who would become heirs of Christ, she was then most free to serve God and most preserved from sin…. The labor pains were part of the punishment connected with original sin. The female was gladly to suffer these steps of procreation and put her trust in God…. since sin came into the world through the female, she could recover her honor by bearing children."[54] In the late nineteenth century, contraception moved from a matter of faith to the realm of government policy. The 1873 Comstock Law (a ban on obscene materials, introduced by an American named Anthony Comstock) made it a crime to send information on sex and birth control through the U.S. mail, and no less a statesman than President Theodore Roosevelt suggested that women who sought to limit family size were committing "race suicide." Interestingly, abortion before "quickening" (a term for the first movements in the womb) was neither a specific crime nor banned by the Catholic Church before 1881. But with tighter legal controls over contraceptive information—let alone services—licensed physicians were reluctant to risk professional disgrace. One immigrant midwife named Ann Lohman, who called herself Madame Restell, worked providing sex education, birth control, and abortions to women of all classes until she was arrested and threatened with a lengthy jail sentence. Preferring death to dishonor, she took her own life in New York in 1878, refusing to rot in prison. Defying the Comstock Laws, willing to accept both temporary exile in Europe and prison time in America, Margaret Sanger stepped in to make birth-control advice available.

Sanger, a nurse who worked with immigrant women throughout New York's Lower East Side, initially circulated birth-control information through her magazine *The Woman Rebel*, which was seized by postal authorities in 1914 and declared illegal. To avoid

---

[54] Robert V. Schnucker, "Elizabethan Birth Control and Puritan Attitudes," reprinted in Robert Rotberg and Theodore Rabb, *Marriage and Fertility.* Princeton University Press, 1980; p.81.

prison, Sanger left the United States for a year, studying the diaphragm at Europe's first birth control-clinic in the Netherlands, then returning to introduce this method to American women. As historian Alice Rossi points out, men weren't even willing to print Sanger's pamphlet, *Family Limitation,* saying it was "a Sing Sing job" for which they'd be arrested: "It had to be done in secret, and the hundred thousand copies had to be wrapped and transported to storage in several cities, waiting for word from her to release them. Her plan was to insure simultaneous, rapid distribution, so that the pamphlets would reach people even after her arrest."[55] Her first clinic, located at 46 Amboy Street in Brooklyn, opened on October 16, 1916. Within a decade, one of her loyal regular patients was my grandmother, Shirley.

The Triumph of Suffrage

Even before they could vote, women challenged their political systems and demanded changes in law. During the fiercest years of nineteenth-century suffrage campaigns, not one but two women ran for President of

[55] Alice Rossi, "The Right to One's Body: Margaret Sanger (1879–1966)," in *The Feminist Papers,* p. 519.

the United States: Victoria Woodhull and Belva Ann Lockwood. Woodhull, a "free love" advcocate who dared to advocate doing away with the institution of marriage, ran as a candidate for the Equal Rights party in 1872. Belva Ann Lockwood was refused admission to law school by both Georgetown University and Columbian College (now George Washington University, where your esteemed author teaches) on the grounds that her presence would distract the male students from their studies. Undaunted by rejection, she ran for President—twice—as the nominee of the Equal Rights Party in 1884 and 1888. She became the first woman lawyer allowed to work before the Supreme Court.

Throughout nearly 80 years of campaigning, between 1840 and 1920, arguments for and against women's suffrage varied. Those women (and men) keenly in favor of votes for women stressed several values: the Enlightenment ideals of individual liberty and rational thought, the concept of democracy and informed citizenship in the United States, and women's maternal interest in the welfare of their children as the state took over education and family issues (as Jane Addams said, "Government is now enlarged housekeeping"). Many nineteenth-century feminists did believe women were different from men—but that women's very differences from men would infuse morality and compassion into the rough world of politics. This view allowed some opponents of woman's suffrage, or "antis," to jeer that women were too emotional and softhearted to lead, that voting would lead to divorce and child neglect, that women did not serve in the military (and thus already had separate roles as citizens), and that the Bible dictated women must not have authority over men. Finally, there were also men who feared women might use the vote to ban alcohol.

As both sides clashed, whether in church meetings or in the streets (there were particularly dynamic strikes and parades in England), the question of women's rights divided entire families. Several countries granted the vote to women before the United States passed the Nineteenth Amendment on August 26, 1920. Between 1893 and 1919, women won the vote in England, Canada, New Zealand, Australia, Germany, Norway, Denmark, and Iceland. Elsewhere, it took decades for women to gain voting rights: not until 1944 (France), 1945 (Italy and Japan), 1950 (India), 1952 (Greece), 1953 (Mexico), 1956 (Egypt), and as late as 1971 in Switzerland.[56]

One historical view is that various governments felt compelled to reward women for their sacrifices and contributions during World War I. However, once passed, the Nineteenth Amendment did not usher in a blizzard of feminist change in America. The postwar backlash against socialists, radicals, and immigrants—and the intense racism of the 1920s—created a climate impeding the unification of women, and attempts at further political activism met with intense resistance by the U.S. government. From World War I onward, any woman who expressed a dissenting view or seemed to criticize the existing political system could be branded a Communist (in the West), or a bourgeois individualist (under communism). Every ideology had a justification for silencing women and a label, either political or sexual, for those who spoke out.

Socialism and World War I

Not all activist women had placed their faith in gaining the vote. Some, like Emma Goldman and Mary Harris "Mother" Jones, were not suffragists, for they so distrusted government they doubted much could be gained by including women in what was already a corrupt system. Mother Jones, once called "the most dangerous woman in America," worked primarily on behalf of men—miners, striking mill workers. As Ronnie Gilbert explains, "For Mother Jones, the ability of middle-class women to speak of women's rights and at the same time ignore the often desperate plight of huge numbers of poor women and children was proof ... that if given the

---

[56] "19th Amendment Anniversary Special," *Time*, August 28, 1995; p. 25.

vote they would not know how to use it effectively."[57] Many working women themselves felt little alliance with more privileged female reformers, who sometimes (with good intentions) tried to limit women's working hours and factory jobs. The right to vote had not necessarily improved conditions for working-class men; the Fifteenth Amendment granted black men the right to vote on paper, but those who attempted to exercise this right were threatened, attacked, even lynched. Thus for many women, the key issue was not suffrage but the daily fight for fair wages. Of course, the intersectionality of all these issues led to what is still a classic debate amongst feminists. What is the main cause of woman's oppressed status—capitalism, patriarchy, or racism?

Inheritance and marriage laws had always complicated adult women's control of money and property, while around the world most women's daily labor was unwaged work—agriculture, collecting firewood and water, housework, child care, food prepara-

---

[57] Ronnie Gilbert, *Ronnie Gilbert on Mother Jones: Face to Face With the Most Dangerous Woman in America.* Berkeley: Conari Press, 1993; p. 31.

tion. As new theories of socialism grew in the late nineteenth century, *socialist feminists* emerged to address what Marxists liked to call "the woman question." Flora Tristan argued that labor was a feminist priority because unless women were fairly paid for waged work, they would have to turn to prostitution. In Russia, Alexandra Kollantai, who would later lead the Woman's Bureau of the Bolshevik Party in 1917, defined female freedom as economic independence from the family unit. The intense ideological debates over who owned women's labor drew in American writer Charlotte Perkins Gilman, who identified as a professional sociologist rather than a socialist—but who argued that women's unpaid household labor was part of the gross national product allowing men to amass greater wealth, and that housework should be professionalized. She also suggested that because women had to attract men and marry in order to survive, marriage itself was a form of prostitution, an exchange of sexual favors for economic security. One convert to American socialism was Helen Keller, whose essay "How I Became a Socialist" appeared in the *New York Call* in November 1912.

It was German socialist Clara Zetkin who founded International Women's Day, first held in 1911 with public parades in countries such as Germany, Austria, Switzerland, and Denmark. During 1911 the plight of working women who were underpaid and forced to do "sweatshop" labor in dangerous conditions gained tragic publicity with New York's Triangle Factory fire on March 25. However, fear of socialism also led to ongoing backlash against women uniting as workers, whether across borders at international conferences or locally through public strikes.

The Great War, as it was called by those who experienced it, changed the lives of every woman it touched—as the Second World War would a few decades later—but it also encompassed the Russian Revolution, so that while the U.S. was allied with Russia until the Allied victory, the postwar mood would separate American and Soviet interests.

During World War I, as the Axis powers invaded or cut off sections of Europe from the British Isles to Russia and the Mediterranean, women were killed, raped, and systematically starved; but

they also found empowerment as ambulance drivers, soldiers, weapons manufacturers, nurses, and (in both England and the United States) as suffragists who continued their protests. Alice Paul and her newly formed National Woman's Party made headlines in the U.S. by picketing the White House in defiance of a wartime ban on antigovernment demonstrations; she was arrested, jailed, and went on a hunger strike, ultimately being force-fed (see the film *Iron Jawed Angels*). In Russia, as more men defected from the Eastern Front, Maria Bochkareva organized a women's fighting unit called the Battalion of Death, and trained over 2,000 women as soldiers ready to replace men.

The new media of film and radio allowed people the world over to glimpse how deadly new instruments such as mustard gas, submarines, and the machine gun could take lives in battle. Public reaction to methods of deadly force added to the global movement of *pacifist feminists* who believed women should oppose war: The first woman in Congress, Representative Jeannette Rankin from Montana, voted against the United States' entry into World War I and spent the next 50 years of her life campaigning for peace. Jane Addams helped form both the Women's Peace Party and the Women's International League for Peace and Freedom; though she eventually won a Nobel Peace Prize in 1931, by 1919 she was on the United States' Military Intelligence list of "Who's Who of Pacifists and Radicals." German Marxist Rosa Luxemburg, who founded the antiwar Spartacist League (later the Communist party of Germany), was imprisoned and then brutally murdered, her body thrown into Berlin's Landwehr Canal.

The Great War caused so many deaths that Russia and Britain in particular faced a "lost generation" of men, making it difficult for women to find husbands and marry. Such demographic shifts, as usual, placed more women into empowered work roles, but out of necessity rather than liberation. Armenian women who had endured assaults from the Turkish forces of the Ottoman Empire (in what is still viewed as genocide in the surviving Armenian diaspora) represented just one tragic dispersal of immigrants and refugees, in addition to multiple Jewish communities fleeing European anti-Semitism. The postwar migration from war-torn Eastern and Southern Europe led to strict new quotas for the U.S. melting pot. Women who struggled to preserve their own cultural traditions often did so in secret—or lost their language, their identities, even their names, as they assimilated into the American landscape.

Between the Wars: Flappers and Film

In the 1920s, a world shaken by war turned to the new art form (and source of escapist entertainment) called cinema, and film promoters learned that the look and style of "movie stars" could be mass-marketed. New, commercialized ideals of beauty were exported globally from Hollywood's dream factory, but only within the limits of moral production codes governing race-mixing and sexuality. Talented black actresses were segregated in "race" films, although many entertainers and blues singers like Gertrude "Ma" Rainey, Billie Holliday, and Bessie Smith found a warm reception through the burgeoning performance venues of the Harlem Renaissance. The creation of a line of beauty products for black women's hair care made Madame C. J. Walker one of the wealthiest African-American entrepreneurs—and a philanthropist who used her fortune to train other black women in business and hair care. During the Prohibition against alcohol in 1920s America, and also in the more open nightclubs of interwar Germany and France, black and white as well as straight and gay women met to drink, dance, and love. Scandalous novels like Radclyffe Hall's *The Well of Loneliness* and the writings of Gertrude Stein introduced lesbian culture into mainstream literary circles. Of course, greater awareness did not equal greater tolerance; in fact, the many independent "spinsters" created by the Great War now faced new scrutiny, and heads of all-female institutions like schools were particularly suspect—a theme explored in playwright Lillian Hellman's *The Children's Hour.* Hostility toward lesbians could now be used to discredit women's organizations or women's aspirations to male halls of power including politics, athletics, and the military. Such tactics continued throughout the rest of the twentieth century and now well into the twenty-first.

The popular image of the 1920s "flapper" conveyed new sexual agency and freedom for young women. Moreover, the daring mood extended to women embracing new inventions and becoming athletes, automobile racers, and pilots. Americans warmed to new heroines: Gertrude Ederle, whose record-breaking swim across the English Channel in 1926 was two hours faster than five previous male swimmers; and solo pilot Amelia Earhart. (Alice Ramsay had already made headlines as the first woman to drive a car coast-to-coast, back in 1909.) But elsewhere during the postwar era, activists continued to push for changes in the paradigm of socially constructed race and gender roles. Ida B. Wells, who had struggled to see black women included in suffrage campaigns and parades, fought tirelessly against the lynching of African-Americans. In *A Room of One's Own* (1929), Virginia Woolf lamented the still-hostile climate for female scholars and writers which so limited female genius, asking, "Let me imagine ... what would have happened had Shakespeare had a wonderfully gifted sister,"[58] and contributing two other famous quotes:

A woman must have money and a room of her own if she is to write fiction.[59]

Women have served all these years as looking glasses possessing the magic and delicious power of reflecting the figure of man at twice its natural size.[60]

Like Mary Wollstonecraft and Charlotte Perkins Gilman before her, Woolf suggested that true economic independence would lessen women's need to fawn over/flatter men. By the 1930s, anthropologist Margaret Mead was making waves with critical analysis of the ways "natural" sex roles were in fact flexible, and quite differently assigned—even reversed—depending on the culture.

After the stock-market crash of 1929, which ushered in a

[58] Virginia Woolf, *A Room of One's Own*. Harcourt, Inc., 1929; p. 48.

[59] Ibid., p. 4.

[60] Ibid., p. 35.

decade of economic depression and hunger, the plight of female migrant laborers became familiar to many through the photography of Dorothea Lange and the writings of John Steinbeck; but not all were sympathetic. One wave of reaction to poverty, overcrowding, and overpopulation was a burgeoning *eugenics movement* banning mixed-race marriages and advocating sterilization of "unfit" women. These policies reached their nadir in the racial laws and genocide of the Holocaust.

War Work, WACS, and the Holocaust

The Second World War tore into women's lives, separating friend from friend and mother from child. Beginning in the mid-1930s, in Hitler's Third Reich, the infamous policies of the Nazi Holocaust sent six million Jews into slave-labor and death camps, sparing neither women nor children—in fact, Jewish women were targeted as dangerous reproducers of an undesirable race, while lesbians (and

German women "guilty" of having sex with Jewish men) were punished in separate camps. Dehumanization of women began with the shaving of their hair, as had once been done during witch trials; other women were used in the medical experiments and acts of sexual sadism rampant in the concentration camps. Where ancient German fairy tales had once warned Hansel and Gretel of an evil witch who would bake them in an oven, this became an unspeakable and horrifying reality as German authorities gassed and burned Jewish children with their mothers.

KOCH ILSE
29 7340

One of the most troubling aspects of women's history is how enthusiastically many German women as well as men embraced fascism, serving as prison guards (Ilse Koch, Irma Grese), as nurses overseeing acts of medical cruelty, as agents of hate-filled propaganda—for women in the Reich benefited from war work at improved wages, similar to the Allies' dependence on female employment. The role of Nazi women is explored further in books, including *Women in the Third Reich* and *He Was My Chief: The Memoirs of Adolf Hitler's Secretary;* regrettably, there are many women alive today who either defend the roles they played as Nazis or are active in the movement to deny the Holocaust.[61] But other women in Germany, Poland, Holland, and occupied Europe worked at great personal risk to hide and rescue Jewish children and other desperate refugees; such acts of heroism are carefully documented through the United States Holocaust Memorial Museum and the tribute to "righteous Gentiles" at Yad Vashem memorial in Israel. One com-

[61] See also Alix Christie, "Guarding the Truth," *Washington Post Magazine,* February 26, 2006; and Mark Potok, "Lying About Auschwitz," in Southern Poverty Law Center's *Intelligence Report,* Winter 2010.

pelling book about a woman who smuggled Jews to safety is Diane Ackerman's *The Zookeeper's Wife*.

Women young and old played pivotal roles in resisting captors and captivity. Irena Sendler worked in the Warsaw Ghetto as a plumber, smuggling infants to safety in her toolbox; rescuing over 2,500 children, she kept the names of those she saved buried in a glass jar in her yard. Jewish women did not go passively into victimization; they organized uprisings, printed flyers, and occasionally bedded Nazi guards to gain information or secure the release of loved ones, as described in the volumes *They Fought Back* and *Sobibor*. Zofia Yamaika, only 14 when she was sent into the Warsaw Ghetto in 1939, ran an illegal youth kitchen and press, escaped to join partisan fighters, and died in the act of gunning down 300 approaching Nazi soldiers; 20 years after her martyrdom she received the highest military award given by the Polish government. Rosa Robota blew up one of the four crematoria at the Birkenau death camp, helping 600 prisoners escape. Trained as a fighter in Palestine, young Hannah Senesh parachuted into occupied Hungary to rescue Jewish prisoners, refusing to give up information after being captured and tortured. Women in France worked in the underground resistance movement; and in occupied Holland, Anne Frank was able to hide and begin her diary due in large part to the effort of family friend Miep Gies. Recalled in the film *The Rape of Europa,* quiet librarian Rose Valland kept meticulous notes on when and where Nazi agents removed precious works of art from museums.

After Japan attacked Pearl Harbor in on December 7, 1941, the United States entered the war and mobilized millions of women to take new opportunities in previously male-only industrial production jobs—at good wages. More than 18 million women took civilian and defense jobs. Norman Rockwell's beloved "Rosie the Riveter" poster, which appeared on the May 29, 1943, cover of *The Saturday Evening Post,* shows a female war worker with muscled arms and rolled-up sleeves taking a lunch break with one foot planted on a ripped copy of Hitler's *Mein Kampf.* (The even more familiar "We Can Do It!" poster by J. Howard Miller was actually not Rosie the Riveter; used by the War Production Committee, the poster was made for Westinghouse.)[62] Industrial managers were directed to maximize the work of new female employees with advice such as this:

"Give every girl an adequate number of rest periods during the day. You have to make some allowances for feminine psychology. A girl has more confidence and is more efficient if she can keep her hair tidied, apply fresh lipstick, and wash her hands … Women are often sensitive; they can't shrug off harsh words the way men do. Never ridicule a woman—it breaks her spirit."[63] These wartime tips ignored key social realities: many women had always worked outside the home, in often brutal factory conditions or as domestic servants, with little regard for their comforts or feelings. Had concern for feminine psychology, or suggested limitations for harsh words or ridicule, ever been applied during slavery or under racial segregation? Was it extended to black women made to use separate bathrooms and cups from those of the white children they cared for?

The movement to maximize women's labor was not without backlash, sexism, or racial tension. However, in the United States, President Franklin Delano Roosevelt had appointed a female Secretary of Labor, Frances Perkins, early in his first term; and Eleanor Roosevelt made an enormous impact as a four-term First Lady both beloved and reviled for her social-justice activism. Already renowned for resigning her membership in the prim D.A.R. (Daughters of the American Revolution) when they refused to allow a concert by black contralto Marian Anderson—and arranging for Anderson to sing at the Lincoln Memorial for a crowd of 75,000 in 1939—Eleanor Roosevelt confronted segregation in war industry through alliances with black leaders like Mary McLeod Bethune, president of the National Council of Negro Women.

With so many men departing for war, women were also needed for noncombat military roles, resulting in the creation of the

---

[62] Penny Colman, *Rosie the Riveter: Women Working on the Home Front in World War II.* Crown, 1995; p. 69.

[63] From "Eleven Tips on Getting More Efficiency Out of Women Employees," *Transportation,* July 1943.

Women's Army Corps, or WACs, and similar branches in the Navy (WAVES) and Air Force (WASPS). Britain, in turn, made use of the WRENs—armed members of the Women's Royal Naval Service. Patriotism permitted new reforms in women's athletics: Made famous by film director Penny Marshall's 1992 hit *A League of Their Own*, the All-American Girls Professional Baseball League fielded teams around Lake Michigan from 1943–1954, offering wartime athletic entertainment that also propelled talented (white) women into sports careers. (Black women, too, played pro baseball, but in the Negro Leagues; Toni Stone and Mamie "Peanut" Johnson were two outstanding players.)

The war years offered few benefits for Asian women under occupation or for Japanese-American women in the United States, who, regardless of being American citizens under the Fourteenth Amendment, were summarily removed from prosperous communities on the West Coast by President Roosevelt's Executive Order 9066 in February 1942, and forced into desert "internment" camps for the duration. The experiences of women in these remote Western camps, trying to sustain family life and the education of their children, were later chronicled in postwar works like Mine Okubo's *Citizen 13360* and Jeanne Wakatsuki Houston's *Farewell to Manzanar*. Much later still, the rape of young Chinese, Japanese and Korean women by Japanese forces, and the abuse of so-called "comfort women" kidnapped for Japanese officers, would emerge through the research of scholars such as Georgetown University's Dr. Bonnie Oh.[64]

With the dropping of the atomic bomb on Japan in August 1945, the end of the Second World War signaled the West's capability of nuclear destruction, and ushered in the era of the arms race. For women's groups dedicated to global peace work, the Holocaust and Hiroshima were terrifying reminders that "advanced" societies did not necessarily value human life, nor protect women and children when other political interests were at stake. Documentary film images and testimony of women who survived or perished in the Nazi death camps, Japanese prison camps, slave-labor factories, and comfort-woman brothels introduced new awareness of female endurance, bravery, and survival skills as war crimes were gradually prosecuted. But the postwar climate of the Cold War and the division between East and West also erected new barriers between American women and women living under communism in the Soviet Union, China, Eastern Europe, and, eventually, North Korea, East Germany, Vietnam, and Cuba. Throughout the 1950s and 60s, women organizing for change in the West could be silenced and discredited with the simple accusation: "Are you some kind of pinko?" Likewise, women questioning expectations of the female role under socialism could be punished for expressing views considered counter-revolutionary. Women were not spared execution if their actions seemed disloyal to their own governments: In the United States,

[64] See *Legacies of the Comfort Women of World War II*. Margaret Stetz and Bonnie B.C. Oh, editors; M. E. Sharpe, 2001.

Ethel Rosenberg, convicted of spying and sentenced to death for treason, died in the electric chair.

The Rosa Parks Bus. Henry Ford Museum, Michigan.

The Postwar/Civil Rights Era

The 1950s era of idealized domesticity has been well-documented in American women's history. After a temporary but life-altering period of war work and shared sacrifices, men and women returned to race and gender roles emphasizing their differences rather than their human similarities. Women who had been valued war workers now lost their union-waged factory jobs and became isolated in the home, resulting in the *baby boom;* black women and men reentered a brutally segregated society which did not extend the G.I. Bill veterans' benefits of college tuition, homebuyers' credits, or loans to nonwhite servicemen. After a hard-won war supposedly fought as a triumph of democracy over fascism, civil rights movements now emerged worldwide: the 1940s saw India gaining independence from British rule and the departure of other colonial powers from Asia and Africa.

Women played critical roles in these independence movements, although too often those advocating female legal empowerment were told that the "woman question" must wait until after the revolution, or that a "true" female revolutionary found liberation only through male-defined struggle. And as postwar refugees competed for security and national homelands, each marginalized group displaced another, resulting in hostilities that are yet to be resolved today: The birth of the modern state of Israel in 1948 was certainly regarded by Palestinian women as the *Naqbah,* or Catastrophe; the partition of India into Pakistan pitted Hindu and Muslim women against one another in bloody confrontation; the division of Ireland into the self-governed Catholic Republic and the British, Protestant-ruled North saw women dead set against one another, block by block, in Belfast.

In South Africa, rather ending decades of Boer and British colonization, the era after World War II saw intensified white control under the brutal new *apartheid* system, which even forbade European and black South African women from sitting on the same city benches. So it was in the American South. As the civil rights movement grew in the United States, it was symbolized by women as varied as Rosa Parks, the first young black women enrolling in whites-only public schools, elderly women beaten and jailed by police, and four small girls murdered in a church bombing in Birmingham, Alabama. Separate bathrooms, drinking fountains, hospitals, schools, and recreation facilities made it unlikely that black and white women would meet beyond the tight boundaries of an employer-servant relationship.

Since keeping a service job required black women to meet the needs of white people with seeming agreeability, many white families were all the more stunned by news images of organized black civil disobedience and, later, violent uprisings. Those white women who joined the civil rights movement in the United States were vilified and investigated, charged with being communist agitators, promiscuous race-mixers, and so forth. But black women risking their lives to challenge Jim Crow law were confronted, daily, by the virulent racism of white women. Interviewed for the film *Freedom Riders* on the 50th anniversary of that action—a mixed-race bus trip through the segregated South in May 1961—former Freedom Rider Catherine Burks-Brooks recalled being surrounded by white women urging their menfolk to kill her. "They were yelling 'Kill the niggers,' and they had *babies in their arms*."

The French philosopher Simone de Beauvoir, one of the few feminist authors widely read during the 1950s, argued that too many people found meaning and identity for themselves by projecting undesired, negative qualities onto a demonized Other. This could be seen in the dichotomy of German/Jew in the Holocaust, and in the race and caste codes of ethnic segregation well beyond the American South. De Beauvoir primarily addressed the ways men had constructed women as an Other: defining themselves as the dominant norm and the female as less human, as lacking masculine attributes. But when women began organizing around the ills of racism in the civil rights era, few saw their own group oppression as women. That consciousness would develop more slowly, in the 1960s and 70s.

The new medium of *television*, though often censored and not available to communities lacking signal reception, brought images of the civil rights movement and its leaders into the home—along with commercial advertisements suggesting that all any woman required to be happy was the right cleanser, rather than social justice. If television reinforced the ideal of women as housewives defined by their consumer habits, it nonetheless broadcast political news, too; news which could be watched while changing a baby (or cleaning another woman's house). More importantly, women isolated in the domestic sphere could now catch ongoing glimpses of how *other women lived*. This inspired some to activism, and others to status-seeking. Girls born in the mid-1950s and thereafter saw television ads urging them to collect (and dress like) Mattel's Barbie doll, the iconic toy introduced by Jewish businesswoman Ruth Handler in 1959. Teen baby boomers embracing beach culture now wore *bikini-style* swimsuits, named for the Pacific island atoll of Bikini where the U.S. conducted atomic bomb tests.

As the 1950s bled into the 1960s, a decade of assassinations and the escalating American war in Southeast Asia, many women turned to antiwar organizing through groups like Women Strike for Peace. They marched against atomic-bomb testing in the American West, which had caused radioactivity in milk sold to their children; they held aloft posters with the famous art slogan developed by Lorraine Schneider, "War is not healthy for children and other living things." Yet as Betty Friedan would soon point out in her 1963 bestseller *The Feminine Mystique,* being an educated mother or former World War II worker did not guarantee that women's concerns would be heard, let alone taken seriously. The female half of the population still lacked political credibility, clout, and representation. But that was about to change.

The Second Wave: Women's Liberation and the Sexual Revolution

What's often referred to as *second-wave feminism* covers so many events, ideas, and people that it continues to generate books, papers, films—and backlash. As women gained a political education through their roles in the civil rights and antiwar movements of the 1960s, many awakened to an analysis of their own status in male-dominated groups. Others who were committed to the ideals promised by American democracy remained frustrated by the limits placed on women's

SOLIDARITY WITH WOMENS STRUGGLES ALL OVER THE WORLD

education and employment, and lobbied for change, beginning with President John F. Kennedy's Commission on the Status of Women and Title VII of the 1964 Civil Rights Act (which outlawed discrimination based on sex). Author/activist Betty Friedan founded the National Organization for Women in 1966, and by 1971 Gloria Steinem was publishing *Ms.* magazine to mass-market feminist journalism. Awakening women around the world to examine their own lives, second-wave feminism splintered into hundreds of causes: birth-control availability and abortion rights; access to child care and women's health information; the need for rape crisis centers and resources for battered wives; access to education where colleges and high schools continued to discriminate against bright women; equal wages and political representation; and an end to belittling images of women in ads and film. Religion, too, had to make some accommodations within these winds of change, with greater freedoms in dress and vocation for Catholic nuns after the 1965 Vatican II Council; America's first female rabbi, Sally Priesand, was ordained in 1972. (The Conservative movement of American Judaism did not ordain its first female rabbi for another 13 years: Amy Eilberg, in 1985. And female rabbis are not recognized by the State of Israel, which defers to Orthodox legal interpretations.)

One key way the *second wave* differed from nineteenth-century feminism's *first wave* was the emphasis on sexual freedom and open expression of female sexuality. This so-called "sexual revolution" offered women greater agency to address formerly suppressed issues such as female desire, lesbian identity, date rape, and workplace harassment—although gradual social acceptance of premarital sex also introduced new risks and avenues of exploitation. With the availability of the birth-control pill after 1960, the movement for reliable contraception and abortion services led to a series of high-profile court cases in the United States, including *Griswold v. Connecticut* in 1965 (which legalized the sale of birth control in all states) and *Roe v. Wade* in 1973 (which legalized abortion).

Yet for all these breakthroughs, change was slow. During the 1960s, the U.S. Congress considered 884 bills on women's rights

and passed just ten. The Equal Rights Amendment failed to be rat-
ified to the U.S. Constitution; women who supported this bill, or
who advocated a pro-choice plank, could be excommunicated or
denied communion by their churches, and both the John Birch Society and Phyllis Schlafly's Eagle Forum argued that female equality was a communist plot. Although three First Ladies (Rosalynn
Carter, Betty Ford, and Lady Bird Johnson) joined the 20,000
American women at the National Women's Conference in Houston, Texas in 1977, mainstream newspapers jeered feminist gath-
erings as "bra-burning" spectacles; no woman delivered the
evening news on network television until the 1980s. And although
1975 was declared the International Year of the Woman—and in
1976 *Time* magazine named "women" its choice for Man of the
Year—in the United States there were more animal shelters for
abused pets than shelters for women and children fleeing domestic violence; and the international peace work led by women in
Northern Ireland (who won the Nobel Peace Prize in 1977) received little press. Throughout the 1970s, only two women were
elected as state governors: Dixy Lee Ray from Washington state,
and Ella Grasso from Connecticut. (Grasso became the first
woman to be reelected for a second term as well.)

Fed up with trying to change the system from within, radical
feminists continued to create women-only spaces and institutions,
from women's presses, bookstores, record companies, and lesbian
music festivals to health clinics, auto repair schools, and self-de-
fense workshops. The ongoing critique of *patriarchy* included
spray-painting offensive billboards and staging public actions
against pornography (including "Take Back the Night" marches
still popular in college towns); a newly trained generation of feminist legal scholars protested the way rape survivors were interro-
gated about their sexual histories in court. Antipornography
activists like Andrea Dworkin charged that demeaning images of
women violated all women's civil rights, and that tolerating the
abuse of women was a key failing of radical men. Why were the
antiwar men of the 1960s slow to oppose *violence against women*
in the 1970s? The question of whether pornography was a form of
free speech, and the image of feminists as antisex due to their ac-

tions against rape and porn, led to debates which feminists call the "sex wars" of the 1980s. By the 1990s, more global attention focused on the sex trafficking of women, which continued as an economic reality well after magazines celebrated "post-feminism"; the introduction of the internet made the marketing of child pornography and the sale of women across borders that much harder to control.

Girl Power/Title IX

Part of female empowerment, and granting women of all ages more control over their bodies, involved expanding access to sports participation. *October, 1973: 6–4, 6–3, 6–3!* This wasn't the secret launch code of a spaceship, but something just as powerful: the winning score of athlete Billie Jean King's victory over Bobby Riggs in a tennis match that rocked the world. A woman could beat a man! March 3, 1976: Yale rower Chris Ernst and 19 other crew women occupied the Yale athletic office to protest their lack of access to basic boathouse facilities. Stripping off their shirts, the rowers presented athletic bodies painted with the words TITLE IX as Ernst declared: "These are the bodies

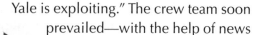

Yale is exploiting." The crew team soon prevailed—with the help of news coverage from around the world. Title IX, an amendment to the U.S. Education Acts of 1972, guaranteed American girls equal opportunity in school sports programs, and the rise of the female athlete ushered in three decades of rapid achievement.

One early women's professional basketball team, the WBL, was started in 1979, with eight teams (including the California Dream). Players were still required to attend charm school. But other victories followed as more and more female athletes dared to break barriers: In 1991, Algerian runner Hassiba Boulmerka became the first woman from an Arab country to win gold in an international track event. Morocco's track star Nawal el Moutawakel became the first Afro-Arab woman to win Olympic gold. At the 2000 Sydney Games, Australia's Cathy Freeman became the first Aboriginal woman to win Olympic gold; at Salt Lake City in 2002, bobsledder Vonetta Flowers became the first African-American, male or female, to win gold in the Winter Games.[65] Soccer player Mia Hamm became a heroine to millions of little girls during the U.S. women's 1999 World Cup victory. Gradually, the Olympics abandoned the insult of *femininity testing* (though questions about gender identity rose after South African runner Caster Semenya's victories in 2009), and allowed women to compete in ice hockey, weightlifting, pole vaulting, and softball. Women from traditional Islamic nations still struggle to participate fully in the Olympics, and recent revelations about socialist governments' steroid experiments on female athletes

[65] Adding to the list of women of color medaling in the Winter Olympics, my own George Washington University women's studies student and athlete Elana Myers won a Bronze in bobsled at Vancouver, 2010.

in the 1970s have left critics suspicious of record-breaking achievements by Olympic women. (The 2008 film *Doping for Gold* shows the degree to which the East German government experimented on young female bodies in order to produce Olympic medalists.)

Political Candidates—Left and Right

The late twentieth century saw a gradual rise in the serious political candidacy of women—as well as the ascendance of women to leadership in postcolonial nations. In the United States, Hawaiian Representative Patsy Mink became the first non-white woman elected to Congress; Shirley Chisholm, in 1969, was the first black woman Representative. A list of female prime ministers since World War II does not, alas, include the United States—although women including Shirley Chisholm (1972) and Hillary Clinton (2008) ran as serious candidates. Most of us have heard of Indira Gandhi, Golda Meir, Benazir Bhutto, and Margaret Thatcher. We are less often directed to recite the names of women who served as prime ministers in Turkey (Tansu Ciller), Poland (Hanna Suchocka), New Zealand (Jenny Shipley, Helen Clark), Senegal (Mame Madior Boye), Jamaica (Portia Simpson-Miller), Iceland (Johanna Sigurdardottir), Norway (Gro Harlem Brundtland), South Korea (Han Myung Sook), Canada (Kim Campbell), Central African Republic (Elisabeth Domitien), Dominica (Mary Eugenia Charles), Sri Lanka (Sirimavo Bandaranaike). Like men appointed or elected in times of political upheaval, some female leaders were assassinated (Bangladesh's Khaleda Zia, Pakistan's Benazir Bhutto, Rwanda's Agathe Uwilingiyimana, India's Indira Gandhi).

"If you want something said, ask a man. If you want something done, ask a woman."

But what startles many students of women's progress is that even now, in 2011, the United States ranks 90th in the world in terms of female representation in government. (And a women's bathroom is only now being added to the men's room conveniently located near the floor of the House of Representatives.) Does the U.S. suffer from a fear of female leadership? Most breakthroughs have been quite recent: Janet Reno was appointed the first woman Attorney General in 1993; Madeleine Albright became the first female secretary of State in 1997; Nancy Pelosi became the first female Speaker of the House in 2007.

Globalizing Feminism

In developing our new Strategic Plan, UN Women has identified women's economic empowerment and women's political participation and leadership as two of our five interrelated thematic priorities—together with ending violence against women and girls, and engaging women fully in peace and post-conflict processes, and in national development planning.... First let me say that the increasing numbers of women in leadership positions is a sign of their empowerment, not a substitute for it.[66]

Today, efforts to provide women and girls with equal opportunity in education and political leadership are at least nominally supported by most countries. After a decade of brutal Taliban repression, Afghanistan elected its first female governor, Habiba Sarabi, in 2005. The ongoing outrage of sexual violence against women has finally been recognized by the United Nations, with broader reporting on rape as an act of intimidation in war. But global practices of female circumcision, entrenched within many Islamic societies (though not supported by Islamic law), present a huge problem for medical and legal authorities across borders: Can public laws eradicate local customs, which are frequently passed along or even performed by women?

Moreover, until economic independence is a reality for all women, it's not feasible to suggest that every woman threatened

---

[66] Michelle Bachelet, Undersecretary General and Executive Director of UN Women, April 28, 2011.

with domestic violence should simply leave her home. Critics point out that we usually expect the victim to leave the house, while the lawbreaker remains in it. A rapist is not always a stranger; where intimate violence is the likeliest threat to a married woman, there's also no point in advising wives to stay inside for their own safety. What's needed is a reliable alternative, a system of support networks, and a means of sustaining abused women and girls beyond temporary shelters or charities.

These are issues which keep a focus on women as *victims,* a perspective that makes many women uncomfortable with feminism and with women's history approaches that seem to dwell on the negative. Female achievement and empowerment are visible, now, as never before. Yet the ease with which basic rights may be taken away was illustrated in 1995 when the Taliban seized power in Afghanistan and promptly closed all schools for girls, threatening even those women who taught their daughters at home. New laws passed in the United States now permit pharmacists in neighborhood drugstores to deny contraceptives to women, even when shown a doctor's prescription. To save money, states like Nevada and North Carolina have proposed axing Women's Studies programs from state-university budgets. How will we learn about our foremothers in the future, secure the autonomy of our very bodies, or make sure girls in every nation have the right to attend school?

Chapter Three

Not All Women's History Looks the Same

Who is a GENERIC WOMAN?

The nineteenth-century notion that women are bound together by common oppression freezes and levels their enormously diverse experience ... oppression, even as women consciously employed the concept, meant different things at different times to different groups and classes of women.... In fact, women have been kept apart in their oppression.
　　　　　　　　　—from *Liberating Women's History* [67]

There's no question that women's history tells a different story from the standard, male-oriented history most of us were taught. But then there are the significant ways that women differ from one another.

How many kinds of *women's history* are there? And which women are represented in the dominant narrative of how "our" foremothers won the vote, ran for office, or took a war job?

The previous chapter offered just one model of a women's history survey course—a sweeping, introductory look at issues and

---

[67] Ann D. Gordon, Mari Jo Buhle, and Nancy Schrom Dye, "The Problem of Women's History," in *Liberating Women's History,* ed. Berenice Carroll. University of Illinois Press, 1976; pp. 86–87.

turning points primarily involving women in the Western heritage, or what's sometimes called the global North. Again, that's a limited framework, one that privileges European and American history at the expense of material from the perspectives of Asian and African women. Feminist scholars trying to piece together the totality of women's experiences throughout history must rely on the contributions of multiple *area specialists*, each bringing a piece of the enormous puzzle to be assembled. It would be a bold scholar indeed who asserted "I'm a women's history specialist" and meant she had expertise in *all* of it, everywhere, through time. But because women's history is a recent (and often misunderstood) field, those operating within in it are expected to represent all women, everywhere.

In reality, early in graduate school or independent research, each historian chooses a concentration in *one area*. For practical purposes, this boils down to working within European, American, Asian, African, Latin American, Native American, or Middle Eastern history. Then there's a choice of time period: Ancient? Medieval? Pre-Columbian? Modern? Colonial? Postcolonial? Finally, will the research focus be based on cultural or political *events* (labor strikes, war, elections, riots, revolutions, rebellions) or *identities* (the history experienced by nuns, schoolteachers, lesbians, or female athletes? And by the way, some women were all four!). Soon, deconstructing *women's* history starts to look pretty complicated. And it should be.

As Elizabeth Spelman argued in *Inessential Woman,* by lumping all women together we lose sight of the very differences which determined women's fates.

> It surely would lighten the tasks of feminism tremendously if we could cut to the quick of women's lives by focusing on some essential "womanness." However, though all women are women, no woman is only a woman. Generic women don't eat rice and beans, collard greens, samosa, challah …

> It was not a generic woman who made at least three hundred trips through the swamps and woods of the Southeastern United States rescuing her people from slavery. It was not some generic women who daily created ways to maintain some shred

of dignity beneath the heels of Nazi boots. It is not generic women who week after week in the Plaza de Mayo bear witness for their disappeared ones. Our mothers, our daughters, our sisters, our lovers, are not generic women. There are no shortcuts through women's lives.[68]

The spiral of women's history takes one ever inward, with different chambers of experience opening up within the nautilus. Let's consider one approach: *regional*. Within each global region we find still more categories of difference. Female power, work, and culture in the ancient Arab world depended upon rank and class; Egypt was not Persia, and Palestine not Libya. Who were the women leaders in each of the different tribal dynasties of precolonial Africa? The Ibo, Taureg, Hausa, Himba, and Xhosa have had differing roles for woman across time. What about China? In Chinese history, a footbound Han wife differed from her yurt-dwelling, horse-riding Mongolian counterpart; a peasant girl bending to plant rice under Maoist collectivization in the 1960s was never seen by the Forbidden City's aged Empress Dowager; and nineteenth-century Chinese lesbian poet Wu Tsao, who was also a Daoist priestess, had a life wildly different from that of stoic businesswoman Nien Cheng— who wrote the prison memoir *Life and Death in Shanghai* after her arrest during the Cultural Revolution of the 1970s.

---

[68] Elizabeth Spelman, *Inessential Woman: Problems of Exclusion in Feminist Thought.* Boston: Beacon Press, 1988; p. 187.

Looking at the Balkan region of Eastern Europe, we place women within the complex history of invasions and religious conquests which resulted in an uneasy coexistence of Muslims, Orthodox Christians, Croatian Catholics, Jews, Roma (gypsies), Turks, and (after World War I) Communists. Alliances and cooperation often flourished in those lands where women traditionally used songs and vocalizations to convey village sorrows and losses. Then, during the Bosnian-Serb conflict of the 1980s, women were turned against one another in the movement called *ethnic cleansing,* and the cruel unfolding of that historical moment was recorded by an 11-year-old girl. Zlata Filipovic's journal, *Zlata's Diary,* described daily life in war-torn Sarajevo, and has been compared to the diary of Anne Frank.

And women's history in South America must include a critical overview of every female role from Incan healer and artist to Amazon tribal shaman, from wife of affluent *caballero* to exploited coca and banana harvester. Chiquita Banana and Carmen Miranda are commercial, Hollywood fantasies of South American womanhood, serving other interests than historical accuracy.

There's no way to cover all of women's history in one volume. But we don't set up men's history as monolithic, with all men alike and getting along; nor do we expect a male scholar with expertise on the life of Abraham Lincoln to offer guest lectures on Polish princes or Masai warriors. So, be prepared to choose thoughtfully from the wondrous buffet of global women's heritage; and likewise be prepared to defend why you have elected a focus on *this* area, or have neglected *that* one. But there are certain themes reappearing in women's history which can be studied in every country, ethnic group, and time period. These include (but aren't limited to) motherhood, household work, and local standards for female sexual behavior.

This chapter suggests some *topical* approaches to women's history, expanding the framework used in Chapter Two, and directing you to further resources. After looking at these topics, it may also become clearer why women have failed to join together as a group throughout history. The endless duties of motherhood and household work prevented most women from getting out of the home sphere to join with any other women, aside from immediate relatives or neighbors. Hierarchies of race, class, sexuality, religion, and family position ranked women above or below one another in any given cultural moment. When I ask my students, on a final exam, to respond to the question *Why haven't women everywhere united together,* I'm instructing them to notice ways women themselves have been complicit in their own oppression: whether by mistreating other women, or by fiercely defending certain traditional values or customs that keep women outside the halls of male power. How do women benefit from "rules" that seem to bind them? Where the bottom line is basic survival—food, protection, security, a stable place for children—many women have accepted and then upheld the rules which chained them.

Looking at Marriage and Motherhood

Starting with the obvious, the core female experience shared by most (but certainly not all) women throughout history is motherhood—usually (but not always) preceded by marriage. Women who did not marry or have children were nonetheless affected by

own their societies' definitions and expectations of proper womanhood, which likely centered around marriageability and reproduction.

Women's history offers infinite ways to explore how marriages were conducted across time, from ancient Babylon to the Inuit of Northern Canada. We can compare courtship rituals and betrothal ceremonies; study the expectations for new brides; collect information on cross-cultural wedding rituals, costumes, and songs. Ideas about the proper husband-and-wife relationship, as well as romantic love, changed from era to era and culture to culture; some traditions have changed very little. A bride in rural Sudan, for instance, is still valued by her worth in cows.

One of the biggest differences in men's and women's history is that from the ancient world to present-day tribal practices, high-status men have been allowed to have more than one wife, without losing respect for being nonmonogamous. In fact, their prestige grows. Sacred legal texts from the Code of Hammurabi to the Bible and Koran describe wealthy men who counted multiple wives as their possessions; the Koran permits men to have up to four wives, but only if the husband is prepared to share his attention without favoritism in a fair and just manner. (How first, second, and third wives handled issues of jealousy, barrenness, and inheritance within households has long fascinated women living in cultures where such practices are rare. As I write, two top-rated television shows in the United States are Big Love and Sister Wives, based on polygamous Mormon families.) Today, in contrast, we see state investigations into charges of polygamy and forced child marriage, stretching from the Western United States to Yemen. This modern trend shows that while most marriage customs originate from tribal or religious practices, marriage eventually came to be regulated by government laws. Examples of such nationalized marriage laws include how many wives one man is allowed to marry, the legal age of marriage for girls and women, and, of course, divorce.

The defiant love expressed by couples forbidden to marry is a popular theme in women's history. It's been dramatized in the romantic tragedy of Shakespeare's *Romeo and Juliet,* but lived out in the actual commitment of the Ladies of Llangollen (late-eighteenth-century Welsh lesbians Lady Eleanor Butler and Sarah Ponsonby), or those couples trapped by laws banning interracial marriage in the United States until the 1967 court case *Loving v. Virginia.* As early as 1663, what is today the state of Maryland passed a law forbidding free English women from marrying black slave men; if they dared love, their children were automatically classified as slaves, and the white woman lost her freedom as well. As Marilyn Yalom reminds us, "Laws against miscegenation, enacted or reenacted in forty-one states, made it a crime for blacks and whites to marry. In fact, South Carolina did not remove the official ban against interracial marriage from its statutes until 1999, and Alabama put off till the year 2000 its referendum to eliminate a similar provision."[69] My parents, a Jew and a Gentile, married against advice and custom in their day. The history of women who married "out" of their identity for love predates, but is symbolized by, the Biblical heroine Ruth, who told her beloved future mother-in-law Naomi, "For whither thou goest, I will go.... Thy people will be my people."

Motherhood and pregnancy have always been political. What mixed messages lie within this one subject! There is sacred motherhood, the sex-

[69] Marilyn Yalom, *A History of the Wife.* New York: Harper-Collins, 2001; p. 193.

less motherhood of Madonna and holy infant; and then there's slave rape, date rape, teen pregnancy, and wartime attacks on women by enemy soldiers. The shaming of women who were forcibly impregnated, during slavery or wartime, historically marginalized the children of those nonconsensual unions—a topic one Georgetown student, Clare Flanagan, addressed in her 2011 women's studies thesis "Biological Warfare: Lessons Learned From Children Born of War-Rape in Bosnia." Flanagan noted that children *inherit the shame of their mother's violation.* This has meant (in other times and places such as occupied France, Vietnam, and Rwanda, not just Bosnia) the ostracizing of both mother and child.

A child's mixed-race appearance symbolically represented the literal invasion of the mother by an outsider. Compounding the horrors of such situations, in Australia (after British colonization), Aboriginal children with white fathers were taken away from their birth mothers and put up for adoption by white families, in an effort to strengthen white supremacy and white bloodlines. Those families torn apart by such official policy became known as the *stolen children* generations. Motherhood is not always honored, and this removal of children from loving parents deemed racially "inferior" occurred in North America as well as Australia, dividing Native American and Native Canadian families throughout the twentieth century. White women, too, had their children taken away in questionable adoption processes set up by homes for "wayward" girls (teen mothers). Ann Fessler's book *The Girls Who Went Away* offers a searing look at how surrendering mothers were exploited by social workers and church systems well into the 1970s.

Six good sources for further reading: Robert Rotberg and Theodore Rabb, *Marriage and Fertility;* Patricia Seed, *To Love, Honor, and Obey in Colonial Mexico: Conflicts Over Marriage Choice, 1574–1821;* Ellen Ross, *Love and Toil: Motherhood in Outcast London, 1870–1918;* Ann Stoler, *Wake Up Little Susie: Single Pregnancy and Race Before Roe v. Wade;* Laurel Thatcher Ulrich, *Good Wives: Images and Reality in the Lives of Women in Northern New England, 1650–1750;* Marilyn Yalom, *A History of the Wife.*

Looking at Housework, Cooking, and Material Culture

Many students find it depressing to pursue research on forced marriage, forced pregnancy, lost honor, lost children. Women's history is emotionally draining in ways other subjects aren't. But rest assured, there are also cheerful approaches to women's history—starting in your own family's kitchen cupboards, where products and tools reveal so much about household evolution. Within households, where much of women's work occurred throughout time, we find many of the true delights of history, attracting the work of anthropologists and archaeologists as well. And interviewing your grandmother is a convenient first step.

The study of household food production and what is called *material culture* (a dignified term for all of our accumulated "stuff") reveals how women lived daily: what they wore, how they ground coffee or prepared mate and tortillas or cooked rice. What utensils were used in your grandmother's kitchen? What skills have women lost in the rush to embrace modern conveniences like the microwave and blender? When I sit down with my own mother, a first-generation American who married into a middle-class family in the late 1950s, I'm overwhelmed by the cooking and kitchen skills she mastered during her first year of marriage. The verbs spill out: How to parboil, julienne, fricassee, render, blanch, poach, deglaze, debone, jell. And those were suburban-housewife skills; my mother was already a generation removed from the knowledge of her own immigrant relatives, women who arrived in Brooklyn knowing how to gut, pluck, preserve, pickle, truss, smoke, can, and brew. However, today plenty of American women still hunt, learning at a young age how to dress the game fowl they bring home. Forty miles from my downtown D.C. office, Amish women in rural Maryland and Pennsylvania are still bringing in harvests traditionally, able to winnow, harrow, plow, prune vineyards, milk cows, make hay.

Women's work at home, food preparation, budgeting, the preservation and storage of vital foodstuffs, was never separate from the larger economy. Globally, women and girls today are burdened with the back-breaking labor delegated to them in traditional cultures from India to Uruguay: tending animals, growing rice, bending over looms. But as Duke University professor Laura Edwards reminds us, "The work that women do to make their lives is not recognized as work."

The skills a good wife brought to marriage are clear in Proverbs 31:19: "She layeth her hands to the distaff and her hands hold the spindle." References to the distaff and spindle, and spinning in general, are replete in the plays and poems of ancient Greece and Rome. On Achill Island, the westernmost tip of Ireland, excavations of a deserted village show that husbands and wives each had their own seat on either side of the cottage fireplace: the man's side held his carved pipes for a quiet smoke at day's end, and what we still call the *distaff side* (meaning the female) held the wife's spinning tools. (A woman's work is never done.) Most Western schoolchildren learn the legend of Sleeping Beauty, who pricked her finger on a haunted spinning wheel and fell into an enchanted sleep. But how many girls, today, know how to spin and card wool?

Then there are the spiritual aspects of kitchen history. The cultural or religious obligations each woman brought to food preparation could isolate her from meeting women outside her own group. The Jewish wife who kept kosher, the Muslim woman obligated to buy and prepare *halal* meat, the vegetarian, the woman unable to eat food prepared and touched by someone of a different caste, the restaurants in the American South (or apartheid South Africa) that only served whites: these are ways to study how food codes have prevented women from uniting. How can women gather to plan if they may not break bread together? Whose bread is accepted? And, in their own homes, women have eaten last, eaten least, and often were required to eat separately from the men of their own group. In traditional Hawaiian culture, men and women could not eat together, and "male" foods like pork and bananas were forbidden to women. Advocating (in 1910!) for a multicultural society where all immigrant women might thrive with equal protection, settlement worker Jane Addams honored women's role in transmitting culture and belief through traditional food preparation:

> A yearning to recover for the household arts something of their early sanctity and meaning arose strongly within me one evening when I was attending a Passover Feast to which I had been invited by a Jewish family in the neighborhood, where the traditional and religious significance of the woman's daily activity was still retained. The kosher food the Jewish mother spread before her family had been prepared according to traditional knowledge and with constant care in the use of utensils; upon her had fallen the responsibility to make all ready according to Mosaic instructions that the great crisis in a religious history might be fittingly set forth.... [70]

One of the earliest published books outlining the skills expected of a good homemaker and cook is Gervase Markham's *The English Housewife,* first published in 1615, and containing such gems as these: "But let our English housewife be a godly, constant, and religious woman, learning from the worthy preacher, and her husband, those examples which she shall with all careful diligence see exercised among her servants."[71] In the endless section *Of Cookery,* we find instructions for thrifty use of every part of a hog after slaughter. For liver pudding (*Another of Liver*): "Take the best hog's liver you can get, and boil it extremely till it be as hard as a stone; then lay it to cool, and, being cold, upon a bread-grater grate it all to powder; then sift it through a fine meal-sieve, and put to it the crumbs of (at least) two penny-loaves of white bread, and boil all in the thickest of sweet cream you have...." For *A blood pudding:* "Take the blood of a hog whilst it is still warm, and steep it in a quart, or more, of great oatmeal grits, and at the end of three days with your hands take the grits out of the blood, and drain them clean."[72]

---

[70] Jane Addams, *Twenty Years at Hull-House.* Macmillan, 1910; p. 175.

[71] Gervase Markham, *The English Housewife,* ed. Michael R. Best. Kingston, Canada: McGill-Queens University Press, 1986; p. 7.

[72] Ibid., pp. 72–73.

Bread-grater? Meal-sieve? Penny-loaf? Thick sweet cream and warm blood conveniently lying around the farmhouse? These snippets of woman's heritage, often detailed in old cookbooks, depict the strength and range of skills required (until very recently) for every woman who was "just a housewife." In his study of *The English Housewife,* editor Michael Best also examines "A lesson for the wife" in John Fitzherbert's 1525 volume, *Boke of Husbandry:*

> When thou art up and ready, then first sweep thy house, dress up thy dish-board, and set all things in good order within thy house; milk thy kine, feed thy calves, sile up they milk, take up thy children and array them, and provide for thy husband's breakfast, dinner, supper, and for they children and servants.... And to ordain corn and malt to the mill, to bake and brew withal when need is.... Thou must make butter and cheese when thou may; serve thy swine, both morning and evening, and give thy pullen meat in the morning, and when time of the year cometh, thou must take heed how thy hen, ducks, and geese do lay, and gather up their eggs.... It is a wife's occupation to winnow all manner of corn, to make malt, wash and wring, to make hay, to shear corn; and in time of need to help her husband to fill the muck wain or dung cart, drive the plough, to load hay, corn, and such other.[73]

Compare this list of housewifely obligations to "The Good Wife's Guide," advice to women from a column in *Housekeeping Monthly,* May 1955. By then, most of the household tasks could be done by machine; clothes spinning in the washing machine while a roast marinated in the oven, water heating as if by magic, dessert defrosting, soothing cocktails mixed in the new blender. The wife's new roles included pleasing, listening, and other means of showing she knew that her husband's comforts mattered above her own.

> Be happy to see him. Greet him with a warm smile and show sincerity in your desire to please him.... Make the evening his. Never complain... Your goal: Try to make sure your home is a place of peace, order, and tranquility where your husband can renew himself in body and spirit.... You have no right to question him. A good wife always knows her place.

---

[73] In Best, Introduction, l-li.

Most interesting of all is the way women throughout history were expected to set up house according to their own cultural customs under extraordinary conditions: while traveling, serving in diplomatic posts, journeying by covered wagon, keeping kosher on tropical islands, cooking for enemy soldiers quartered in their own homes, setting up house as wives of Arctic explorers. On this last point, Canadian writer Sheila Burnford (who wrote *One Woman's Arctic,* as well as the classic animal story *The Incredible Journey*) provides a hilarious breakdown of recipes from the *Northern Cookery Book* compiled by white Canadian women stationed on Baffin Island, near the Arctic Circle, in the nineteenth century.

> **Boiled Smoked Beaver came as a relaxed and leisurely miracle: "Smoke the beaver for a day or two, then cut up the meat and boil until it is done."... But Boiled Reindeer Head had the most appeal for me, for all one's ill nature at the prospect of preparing a meal could be vented in the therapy of its preparation. All one needs, beside the reindeer head, is an ax and some cold water. "Skin the head. Then chop it in quarters, splitting it between the eyes with an axe. Cover with cold water and boil until soft."[74]**

Old cookbooks often reveal more social history than edible recipes; on a hotel bookshelf I once found a male-authored food guide that began with the casual instruction, "Have your woman fetch water."

Six good sources for further reading: Hannah Glesse, *The Art of Cookery, Made Plain and Easy,* 1805; *Practical Housekeeping: Careful Compilation of Tried and Approved Recipes,* 1876; Isabella Beeton, *Mrs. Beeton's Book of Household Management,* 1861; Laura Shapiro, *Something From the Oven;* Ruth Schwartz Cowan, *More Work for Mother;* Kathryn Sklar, *Catharine Beecher: A Study in Domesticity.*

Looking at Servants, Slaves, and Labor

Within households throughout history, women's work was performed by various different women, not just one alone. The ex-

---

[74] Sheila Burnford, *One Woman's Arctic.* Atlantic Monthly/Little, Brown and Co., 1972; p. 110.

tended household, ranging across time and place from ancient Israel to colonial Mexico to the Ming Dynasty in China, usually included several generations of female relations, plus servants or even slaves. The reigning female matron (often a mother-in-law to a brutalized new bride, by the way) delegated tasks as well as carrying out certain roles herself. We see this in the Bible's Proverbs 31: *A woman of valor, who can find?* "She flexes her arms.... She rises while it is still night and gives food to her household, *and a portion to her maids*" (my emphasis). Even in non-elite households, caste systems and racial laws made female servants affordable as bonded labor. Therefore an important part of women's history is the phenomenon of women ordering lower-ranked women and girls to do "women's work." Anything considered a wife's responsibility could be delegated to a maidservant: cooking, child care, even the mothering job of breast feeding. Women who lacked political rights or freedoms outside the home could freely indulge in abuses of power within the home, and this has a great deal to do with the lack of trust between women across time.

Working outside the home should never be equated with "liberation," as too often women ended up in unwaged, low-wage, or enslaved and indentured labor. This is a constant theme in women's history: Work does not automatically lead to power, for anyone. Many parents willingly sent extra unmarried daughters out to work in household service or factory labor. Describing industrialization in mid-nineteenth-century France, historians Joan Scott and Louise Tilly explained that "A daughter's departure served not only to relieve the family of the burden of supporting her, but it might help support the family as well. A daughter working as a servant, seamstress, or factory operative became an arm of the family economy."[75] After the Irish potato famine, unmarried women and girls came to the United States in greater numbers than Irish men, competing with newly freed slave women for low-wage domestic work. Because slavery had been legal in the United States for 244 years, the work once associated with

[75] Louise A. Tilly and Joan W. Scott, *Women, Work, and Family*. Holt. Rinehart and Winston, 1978; p. 109.

female slave labor continued to be low-status and barely waged; to this day, stereotyped images of a cheerful "mammy" figure eager to wait on white families may be seen in ads for Aunt Jemima pancake mix.

As women's work moved outside the home, into textile factories and mills, it was badly paid, which led to conflicts with male labor organizers who saw women's wages driving down the minimum payscale for men. Women were certainly not welcome in labor unions until well into the twentieth century, and unions (or Social Security) never existed for the vast majority of women in slavery and/or domestic work, vulnerable to the whims of their mistresses. As men's work became established in the public sphere, women's household work at home was less and less seen or valued—although it didn't grow easier. Devices intended to ease the strain of housework, such as washing machines, soon became high-end status symbols not all women could afford; and upper-class women continued to do neither work outside the home nor "women's work" *in* the home—instead, using servants for those tasks. Finally, Ruth Schwartz Cowan reminds us that technology eased men's household chores more than it replaced women's work:

> In almost every aspect of household work, industrialization served to eliminate the work that men (and children) had once been assigned to do, while at the same time leaving the work of women either untouched or even augmented…. The growth of the meat-packing industry, coupled with the introduction of refrigerated transport in the 1870s and 1880s, meant that men no longer spent much time in butchering. Virtually all of the stereotypically male household occupations were eliminated by technological and economic innovations during the nineteenth century…. But not so with the occupations of women.[76]

[76] Ruth Schwartz Cowan, *More Work For Mother*. New York: Basic Books, 1983; pp. 63-64.

Seven good sources for further reading: Alice Clark, *Working Life of Women in the Seventeenth Century;* Elizabeth Fox-Genovese, *Female Relations in the Plantation Household;* Jacqueline Jones, *Labor of Love, Labor of Sorrow: Black Women, Work, and the Family from Slavery to the Present;* Ivy Pinchbeck, *Women Workers and the Industrial Revolution, 1750-1850;* Ruth Schwartz Cowan, *More Work for Mother;* Kathryn Stockett, *The Help;* Louise Tilly and Joan Scott, *Women, Work, and Family.*

Looking at Artists, Inventors, Daring Women, and Female Genius

So far, all of the preceding background points to one conclusion: Few women had any free time to call their own. (And, politically speaking, few had time to think about the condition of women in general.) Those with artistic yearnings applied their talents directly to objects for daily use: making quilts, designing beautiful cakes and breads, painting or dyeing Easter eggs, applying designs to their own bodies or hair. Because women worked with household objects, those *inventions* emerging from a female hand were likely to be household-related. Thus it was Catherine Littlefield Greene, who worked in Eli Whitney's household, and not Whitney himself who developed the first working model of the cotton gin. The patent went to Whitney because it was not seen as appropriate, in 1793, for a woman to call attention to herself with a patent in her own name.

Women like Greene (and, later, Marie Curie) are sometimes held to different standards than male inventors for other reasons. Without question, the cotton gin brought misery to millions of other (enslaved) women as it made rapid harvesting possible and super-profitable, resulting in the King Cotton economy of the slave South just when the importation of slaves was supposed to be abolished by America law. Curie's research on radiation helped paved the way for atomic warfare. Should women be held accountable for the unsavory uses of their discoveries? Is this another aspect of the woman-blaming trend seen in history?

Women in science, like astronomer Maria Mitchell, were usually well-educated by their fathers or male mentors. But they also found support through women's institutions: After becoming the first woman elected to the American Academy of Arts and Sciences in 1848, Mitchell was an astronomy professor (and director of the observatory) at Vassar College in 1865. At that time, women's colleges offering a curriculum in the sciences defied medical beliefs that the study of "male" subjects like astronomy or physics would cause infertility in young women. Mitchell, who demanded a raise in salary when she discovered she was paid less than younger male professors, was forward-thinking in other ways. In a unique twist which connects her with Catherine Littlefield Greene, the astronomer (and abolitionist) Mitchell showed her opposition to American slavery by refusing to wear cotton-based clothing—which would have been one of the few comfortable fabrics for a heavily covered woman of the nineteenth century.

The struggle to gain the kind of higher education available to ambitious men sometimes forced other female scientists into unusual career choices. Pushed out of the NASA astronaut space program because she lacked a Ph.D., in 1977 Janet Guthrie became the first woman to drive a race car in the Indianapolis 500. Female explorers could sometimes be banned from an entire continent: after the signing of the Antarctic Treaty, women were not allowed at research stations of Antarctica. This policy was broken first by Russian marine geologist Marie Klenova in 1956, and then a team of four Argentine women in 1969: Professors Irene Bernasconi, Maria Adela Caria, Elena Martinez Fontes, and Carmen Pujals.

American women scientists demanding access to the U.S. research station were refused by the commander of the National Science Foundation program, Naval Rear Admiral Fred E. Bakutis, who said the Navy "would be asking for trouble" if women were permitted in Antarctica.[77]

Women in the arts faced unusual biases throughout history, such as the refusal of symphony orchestras to hire women as either musicians or conductors—challenges familiar twentieth-century conductors Antonia Brico and Sarah Caldwell. Racism caused the name of black child prodigy Philippa Schuyler to be less familiar to us than chess prodigy Bobby Fischer. Reading at two and playing the piano at three, Schuyler composed her first symphony, *Manhattan Nocturne,* at thirteen; it was performed at Carnegie Hall by the New York Philharmonic in the mid-1940s. A black woman was not awarded the Pulitzer Prize for fiction until 1983 (Alice Walker, for *The Color Purple);* in that same year Toni Morrison became the first African-American, male or female, to win the Nobel prize for literature. These breakthroughs in the arts were slowly followed by scientific advances as Dr. Mae Jemison became the first black woman astronaut in NASA in 1988.

Despite the plethora of actresses and "starlets" in Hollywood history, filmmaking has continued to be one of the most occupationally segregated professions for over a hundred years. The first

---

[77] Barbara Land, *The New Explorers.* New York: Dodd, Mead & Co., 1981; pp. 16–21.

woman to win an Academy Award for Best Director was Kathryn Bigelow, for *The Hurt Locker*—in 2010. Women have struggled to gain roles behind the camera and in film technology (as light and sound designers, camera crew, gaffers); those who did make films in the twentieth century were often vilified for their participation in propaganda (like Nazi filmmaker Leni Riefenstahl), or censored for being too controversial (like visionary lesbian filmmaker Barbara Hammer).

Six good sources for further reading: Rachel Abramowitz, *Is that a Gun in Your Pocket?*; Stephen Bach, *Leni: The Life and Work of Leni Riefenstahl*; Judy Chicago, *Through the Flower*; Angela Davis, *Blues Legacies and Black Feminism*; The Guerrilla Girls, *The Guerrilla Girls' Bedside Companion to the History of Western Art*; Virginia Woolf, *A Room of One's Own*.

Looking at Indigenous and Aboriginal Women Before Colonization

After the overthrow of Queen Liliuokalani, Sanford Dole's regime passed a law in 1896 stating: "The English language shall be the medium and basis of instruction in all public and private schools." Hawaiian was not taught, and many schools prohibited speaking it, and students were punished for doing so well past statehood.[78]

This one passage tells us a great deal about how indigenous women's words were systematically silenced by colonists and missionaries, who imposed their own laws of language. How do we rediscover the knowledge, work, art, scientific discovery, household inventions, agricultural innovations, and political leadership contributed by women, but lost to us because of the erasures of colonization? The oldest calendar in the Northern Hemisphere was made by women: the Anasazi of Chaco Canyon, who built

[78] Sarah Vowell, *Unfamiliar Fishes*, p. 138.

their pueblos and the nine-circle Sun Dagger petroglyph around 1000 C.E.[79]

Most of the history of *colonization,* including European efforts to Christianize "natives," begins after the voyages of Christopher Columbus—hence the term *pre-Columbian* for civilizations thriving in North and South America before white settlement.

In 1493, just one year after Columbus sailed to the New World, the Pope directed Spanish explorers to "Christianize the New World … that barbarous nations be overthrown and brought to the faith."[80] This command came in the form of a papal bull called *Inter caetera.* Later on, after the Protestant Reformation, other missionaries rushed to compete against Catholic influences, dividing up the native communities of Canada. Last but certainly not least, Mormon teachings declared that Native Americans were in fact descendents of the twelve lost tribes of Israel, and Mormon missionaries moved to make Hawaii and Polynesia (and, later, Madagascar) their own stronghold. Key to seeding new faith practices in each region was the defeat of matriarchal systems granting women authority over men. And the establishment of mission schools, whether Catholic or Protestant, generally involved banning traditional language, dress, hairstyle, faith practices, dances, song, and other customs perceived

[79] The petroglyph was rediscovered by a woman, too: Anna Sofer, in 1979.

[80] Ibid., 151.

as "heathen." This effectively destroyed the tribal traditions once passed from mother to daughter, and as white control tightened, new laws passed to grant or deny benefits to indigenous women who married white men. In the cruel language of Canadian law, such women lost their tribal identity and became "non-status." Indian Acts both in Canada and the U.S. gave men sole possession of property, despite long traditions of female ownership and authority:

> From 1869 until 1985 the determination of Indian status was determined by a patrilineal system; that is, by a person's relationship to "a male person who is a direct descendent in the male line of a male person...." When she married a non-status man, an Indian woman born with status lost it, unable to regain it even if she subsequently was divorced or widowed ... the woman lost her band membership and with it, her property, inheritance, residency, burial, medical, educational and voting rights on the reserve. In direct contrast, an Indian man bestowed his status upon his white wife and their children.[81]

We know that in other regions affected by white rule, such as Australia and New Zealand, aboriginal women were sometimes unable to defend land rights and entitlements because of customs that forbade revealing information to outsiders. The gradual losses of property and relegation to reserved tracts of land or villages isolated and impoverished women (and men), making their cultural contributions and inherited authority less and less invisible to the encroaching white population—and leaving their histories out of the systems of knowledge taught as state-sanctioned education.

Eight good sources for further reading: Diane Bell, *Daughters of the Dreaming* and *Ngarrindjeri Wurruwarrin;* Mona Etienne and Eleanor Leacock, *Women and Colonization,* 1980; Doris Pilkington Garmara, *Follow the Rabbit-proof Fence;* Kathie Irwin and Irihapeti Ramsden, *Toi Wahine;* Nympha Byrne and Camille, *It's Like the Legend: Innu Women's Voices,* 2000; Steve Wall, *Wisdom's Daughters: Conversation of Women Elders of Native America,* 1993; Janet Silman, ed., *Enough is Enough: Aboriginal Women Speak Out,* 1987.

---

[81] Janet Silman, *Enough is Enough: Aboriginal Women Speak Out.* Toronto, Canada: The Women's Press, 1987; p. 12.

Looking at African History and Racial Categorization

The history of women in Africa, too, has primarily been presented through the lens of white critics, well-intended or otherwise. (One web search for "famous women from Africa" directs you to white South African actress Charlize Theron.) Where whites have encountered and described African culture, such histories are bound to contain built-in biases of their time.

The return of Sarah Baartman's remains to South Africa in March 2002 signified the end to a long era of white scientific control over this one, symbolic female African body: at her funeral, South African President Thabo Mbeki "quoted Baron Georges Couvier, a French scientist who dissected Baartman's body after her death, as saying, 'Her moves had something that reminded one of the monkey and her external genitalia recalled those of the orangutang.'"[82] This one story exemplifies the constant debasement of African women by comparing them to animals, especially in terms of their sexuality, in historical eras when white women were assumed to be proper and rigid with regard to sexual appearance and behavior. By exploiting Western curiosity about racial difference, Western scientists were able to construct a dominant narrative of African females as primitive (but sexy: of interest to white men), while African men were portrayed in the white media as primitive (but carnal: a threat to white women). Sadly, educated white women also helped to perpetuate such racist animalism, even today still comparing African-Americans to monkeys, as we see in many of the attacks on President Barack Obama. A 2011 mass email sent by elected political official Marilyn Davenport showed three

Everybody who knows me says they can't believe people are calling me a racist. I am not a racist, but I do think I need to apologize again with different words.

Yup!

[82] *South African News*, August, 9 2002.

chimpanzees—male and female adults, and a baby chimp with Obama's face—with the message: "Now you know why no birth certificate."[83]

Lost in the endless "discovery" of Africa was authentic African history, the reign of queens from Egypt to Ethiopia and southward. The Queen of Sheba may be familiar from the Bible's account of her connection to King Solomon, but other histories of African womanhood are just beginning to be taught in the West. However, it's also essential that Western students grasp the full implication of legal boundaries emerging from the slave trade, and how fears of race-mixing dominated every aspect of American life from school enrollment to swimming lessons right up to the present date. These legal codes, more than any other factor, prevented black and white women and girls from meeting socially, let alone organizing politically. African-American children, for example, were even banned from the annual White House Easter-egg roll until First Lady Mamie Eisenhower protested their exclusion in 1953.

The rise and fall of apartheid in South Africa and the roles black, white, and colored women played during those decades offers a parallel to the history of segregation in the West. We can also look at an entire history of women's literature on the moral problems of the slave trade, books, and speeches circulated from the seventeenth century onward. In 1688, Aphra Behn published the first novel in English by a woman: *Oroonka, or the History of the Royal Slave.*

Seven good sources for further reading: Iris Berger, *Threads of Solidarity: Women in South African Industry, 1900-1980;* Clifton Crais and Pamela Scully, *Sara Baartman and the Hottentot Venus: A Ghost Story and Biography;* Annette Gordon-Reed, *Thomas Jefferson and Sally Hemmings: An American Controversy;* Nancy Rose Hunt, *Gendered Colonialisms in African History;* Jennifer Morgan, *Laboring Women: Reproduction and Gender in New World Slavery;* Dorothy Roberts, *Killing the Black Body;* Rebecca Skloot, *The Immortal Life of Henrietta Lacks.*

---

[83] Colbert King, "The Season of Smearing Obama." *Washington Post,* April 30, 2011.

Looking at Women in Muslim and Jewish History

Jewish and Muslim women share far more than what separates them historically: not only tribal roots and similar customs, but also (and far too often) a history of being persecuted or driven underground for not being Christian. It's important to remember that today's tensions over the role of modern Israel are but a recent conflict; Judaism and Islam began in the same region and both produced strong female leaders, from Deborah to Fatima. And both faiths ended up dispersed globally, far from the Mediterranean, due in part to the destruction of the Jews' second Temple in 70 c.e. and the expulsion of resettled Jews and Moors from Spain by Queen Isabella in 1492. Whether threatened by holy war, Crusades, pogrom, or Holocaust, Jewish women's lives had to adapt to whichever region and culture offered a tolerant home base. Thus the Diaspora of Jewish life developed in multiple languages: Arabic, Ladino, Yiddish, English. In Spain, terrified of discovery during the Inquisition era of the early sixteenth century, both Jewish and Moorish (Muslim) housewives who practiced their faith in secret had to keep a bit of pork hanging on the outer perimeter of the house as a sign the family had converted to Christianity—just one way that women's manipulation of foodways ensured survival in times of attack.

It's also important to understand that, historically, while Islam began amongst peoples we call Arab today, it is no longer a religion of Arabs alone but practiced by Turks, Persians (Iranians), Albanians, Malaysians, black Africans, Chinese Uighurs, the Uzbek and Tajik of Central Asia, and—in the largest Muslim nation in the world—Indonesians. The ways women function as Muslims or Jews in each site depends, as always, on regional history. But one of the key similarities of Islam and Judaism are strict dietary laws: to eat only kosher or halal meat slaughtered ritually, to abstain from pork, to abstain from alcohol (in Islam), and to observe fast days. These expectations across history set up two challenges for observant wives: the near-impossibility of eating with women of a dif-

ferent faith, and the constant effort of keeping house in accordance with purity laws—both dietary and sexual. In fact, one of the barriers to modernizing gender codes in Islam and Judaism is the importance of *separation* in both faiths: separating the permitted from the forbidden, the regular weekdays from the holy day of rest, male from female, pure from impure. When new modernizations and conveniences have been introduced, they haven't always benefitted women; Dawn Chatty has written extensively on what happened when the Bedouin began using trucks instead of camels. Camel-tending had been a women's job, one of the chief ways women met one another to exchange information at wells. But truck-driving, ownership, and repair became exclusively male privileges, reducing female agency.

Women in both Judaism and Islam had important, public roles, particularly as wives entrusted with business transactions. Within the Ottoman Empire, women served as powerful regents in the sixteenth and seventeenth centuries; the daughter of Suleyman I supposedly paid for 400 warships to attack and occupy the island of Malta.[84] In *The Hidden Face of Eve,* groundbreaking Egyptian feminist Nawal el Saadawi reminds us that books advocating the education and liberation of women were being produced in the Arab world in the nineteenth and early twentieth centuries: *A Guide to the Education of Girls and Boys,* published in 1872 by Rifa'a Rafi'i El Tahtawi; *Tehrir El Mara'a* (Liberation of Women) in 1900, and *El Mara'a El Guedida* (The New Woman) in 1911, both by Kassim Ameen.[85] Similarly, women in the ultra-Orthodox Hasidic communities of Eastern Europe life before the Holocaust gradually developed their own educational institutions through the tireless advocacy of a seamstress from Cracow named Sarah Schenierer. As Jews immigrated to the United States in huge numbers between the 1880s and World War II, American Jewish women would play key roles in feminist movements: think of Betty Friedan, Gloria Steinem, Bella Abzug; authors Adrienne Rich, Lillian Faderman, Gerda Lerner; and the first two lesbian folk musicians to produce albums, Maxine Feldman and Alix Dobkin. And while voters in the United States shied away from female candidates, in the rest of the world Jewish and Muslim women emerged as political rulers: Golda Meir served as Prime Minister of Israel, Benazir Bhutto in Pakistan, and Tansu Ciller in Turkey; from Palestine, bold Hanan Ashrawi negotiated with Israel and the West.

Where individual states have elected to follow traditional religious law, we do find limitations on women. In Israel, a secular

---

[84] Ian Dengler, "Turkish Women in the Ottoman Empire," in Lois Beck and Nikki Keddie's *Women in the Muslim World.* Harvard University Press, 1978; p. 237.

[85] Nawal el Saadawi, *The Hidden Face of Eve.* Boston: Beacon Press, 1980; pp. 170–71.

state yet governed by Orthodox Jewish rulings on family laws, no woman may divorce without her husband's agreement, called a *get*. Saudi Arabia is well known for a particularly strict version of Islam, Wahabism, dating only from the eighteenth century, but as Nikki Keddie points out, "Oil income allowed the Saudis, after World War II, to promote their version of Islam through the creation of schools, mosques, and other institutions throughout the world."[86] Islamic revolutions in Iran and Afghanistan reintroduced restrictions on women's social, political, and work choices, mandating the veil and *burqa*.

Elsewhere, as in Algeria and Palestine (and in the Zionist movement, too), the call to women's awakening might be nationalist rather than religious. One rare volume of revolutionary materials edited by a woman, Leila Kadi, quotes male Palestinian Liberation Organization leaders in 1969 praising "the role of the Palestinian woman, which has reached the level of armed resistance."[87] Like many male activists before them, such men believed that women's liberation would come automatically with the end of occupation, and urged women to sacrifice their lives for the nationalist cause if they desired feminism: "National armed struggle always achieves real equality between men and women." (Alas, this was certainly not true after the American Revolution!) Regrettably, today's Western media have seized upon the image of the female commando "Arab terrorist" and suicide bomber—even while fostering simultaneous stereotypes of veiled, passive Muslim women. Digging through such stock images to find real women's history is a challenge. More optimistically, alliances between Israeli, Palestinian, and Western women through the peace-activist group Women in Black points to a desire for conflict resolution led by women, a recent history explored in Ayala Emmett's book *Our Sister's Promised Land*.

---

[86] Nikki Keddie, *Women in the Middle East*. Princeton University Press, 2007, p. 149.

[87] Leila S. Kadi, ed. *Basic Political Documents of the Armed Palestinian Resistance Movement*. Beirut, Lebanon: Palestinian Liberation Organization Research Center, December 1969; pp. 72–3.

Twelve good sources for further reading: Bernadette Brooten, *Women Leaders in the Ancient Synagogue;* Phyllis Chesler and Rivka Haut, *Women at the Wall;* Miriam Cooke and Margot Badran, *Opening the Gate: A Century of Arab Feminist Writings;* Isabel Delloye, *Women of Afghanistan;* Gluckel, *The Memoirs of Gluckel of Hameln;* Paula Hyman, *Jewish Women in America;* Nikki R. Keddie, *Women in the Middle East: Past and Present;* Fatima Mernissi, *Beyond the Veil;* Annelies Moors, *Women, Property and Islam: Palestinian Experiences, 1920-1900;* Afsaneh Najmabadi, *Women's Autobiographies in Iran;* Judith Plaskow, *Standing Again at Sinai;* Nawal el Sadaawi, *The Hidden Face of Eve;* Marjane Satrapi, *Persepolis.*

Looking at Women in Asian Dynasties and "Orientalism"

The history of women in East and South Asia has been shaped by various male viewpoints: local religious ideals for female obedience, and Western fascination with what is called *Orientalism*— stereotypes projecting an exotic, passive, or servile Otherness onto the Asian female. In the patriarchal Confucian tradition, women were subject to the Three Obediences: A woman was to be dominated by her father in childhood, her husband in marriage, and finally by

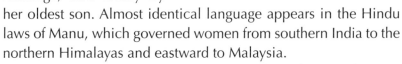

her oldest son. Almost identical language appears in the Hindu laws of Manu, which governed women from southern India to the northern Himalayas and eastward to Malaysia.

Women of what is now Vietnam were also subject to the Four

143

Virtues: told to "work hard, care for their physical appearance, use appropriate speech, master proper behavior."[88] But Vietnamese history also presents a warrior heroine named Lady Trieu who battled the Chinese in war in 248 C.E.—a heroine supposedly nine feet tall with breasts that had to be lifted over her shoulder. (This story is surprisingly similar to the myth of the Greek Amazon warrior, whose breasts get in the way of her bow and arrow competency.)

Depending upon region and dynasty, Asian women were active as warriors and empresses throughout history, hardly the passive sexual objects fantasized by Western men. Unfortunately, with the spread of communism to mainland China, Vietnam, and then Cambodia in post-World War II era, new images rose in the West of the Asian woman as sexless guerilla warrior, whose stoic expression belied the threat she posed to white males. These images had already proliferated in Western film, in policies directing Japanese-American women and infants to be interned in U.S. concentration camps during World War II, and in the U.S. military's treatment of village women and girls suspected of being Viet Cong.

During China's transition to the Communist rule of Chairman Mao, women were told they "held up half the sky," but their liberation came in the form of new work roles and ideological expectations. Punishments could be cruelly carried out by other women empowered by the Party to uphold rigid interpretations of class struggle and belief. During the era of the Cultural Revolution in the 1960s and early 1970s, Madame Mao was frequently far more doctrinaire and punitive than her husband, Mao Zedong, ordering millions into prisons or reeducation labor assignments.

Georgetown University is one of the few American colleges with a focus on Korean studies and a women's studies program directed by a Korean feminist scholar: Dr. Bonnie Oh (now retired; the program continues to benefit from the capstone courses taught by Dr. You-Me Park). Georgetown's new LGBT Center has also grown under the capable leadership of a South Asian feminist, Sivagami Subbaraman from India. In such ways, students in the nation's capital are gently reminded of the fierceness of Asian feminism.

---

[88] Sandra Taylor, *Vietnamese Women at War: Fighting For Ho Chi Minh and the Revolution*. Lawrence, KS: University of Kansas, 1999; p. 20.

Looking at Lesbians and other Sexual Outlaws

Virginia Woolf, who had a love affair with at least one woman, once pointed out that female unity and friendship are rarely depicted in fiction. One of the great tragedies of history is that women have been set against one another, in countless ways, even as they were forbidden entry to male [public] spaces and restricted to feminine [private] environments. Segregated by law or custom into same-sex schools and female subcultures, where they nurtured important and loving companionships, women were nonetheless directed toward the end goal of marriage and learned to compete for men, male attention, and male approval in unhealthy ways. One tactic discouraging women from making other choices, or from building sympathetic alliances with other women, was the threat of a *bad reputation*. And a *good reputation* was almost always based on ideals of proper sexual behavior and identity, dictated by men who ranged from celibate clergy to medical doctors to police.

The separation of *good* woman from *bad,* lady from harlot, and hetero from homo has dictated laws and attitudes in every era, simply expressed in different words (slut, tommie, incorrigible, bulldagger, invert, goodtime girl). Prostitutes, fast girls, "manly" women suspected of lesbianism, and women who temporarily passed or lived their entire lives as men have true histories of their own—apart from their unflattering depictions in religious, psychological, and criminal records. We know that women loved women from Biblical passages condemning such behavior; we know that women sold their sexual services to men from the first written laws, the Code of Hammurabi in ancient Babylon. Indeed, sex work is

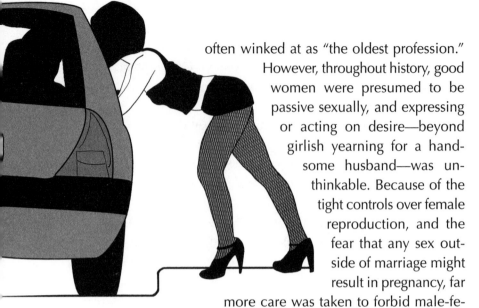

often winked at as "the oldest profession." However, throughout history, good women were presumed to be passive sexually, and expressing or acting on desire—beyond girlish yearning for a handsome husband—was unthinkable. Because of the tight controls over female reproduction, and the fear that any sex outside of marriage might result in pregnancy, far more care was taken to forbid male-female interactions and to guide proper heterosexual behaviors. What two women did together attracted less concern, for it did not result in children or, technically, "deflower" a virgin—she could still marry well. In contrast, *sodomy laws* punishing men for homosexual sex acts were part of most early nation-states, often linked to disapproval toward the man who appeared effeminate or willingly took on the lower-status female role in coupling.

When does lesbian history begin? Historians may start with Sappho, but of course same-sex relationships existed in every culture before and since her one life on the Greek island of Lesbos. A contentious issue is how we identify women in history who may have had life partnerships with women, but who probably did not think of themselves in modern terms we use (gay, lesbian, bi, queer, trans, dyke, invert; there are hundreds of phrases). When did a lesbian consciousness begin? When did women become aware there were other women who preferred women—even a global community, across time? When did a lesbian-rights movement first emerge?

The best scholar in this area is Lillian Faderman, who addressed many of these questions in her book, *Surpassing the Love of Men: Romantic Friendship and Love Between Women from the Renaissance to the Present*. A brilliant and prolific historian, Faderman explains that women in the past, while assumed to be disinterested in marital sex, were also tolerated as more emotional and "sentimental" than men—meaning they could hug, kiss, express affection with one another, and not attract much attention. It was heterosexual activity that was explicitly taboo for women—being caught with a man.

Carroll Smith-Rosenberg also examines this history of gushing friendships in her famous essay, "The Female World of Love and Ritual." In fact, the general belief was that sex had not occurred unless a man's penis was involved; male penetration—of a female or another male—was the serious act, especially the perforation of a virgin's hymen. Women who were socially outcast and persecuted, Faderman explains, included those who assumed male roles and male privileges for themselves: working-class butches, women who passed as men, and at the other end of the class spectrum, wealthy women who refused to marry or reproduce male heirs, preferring female companions. "In the seventeenth century Christina of Sweden, who dressed in men's clothing even while on the throne, abdicated in order not to marry. She settled for a time in Paris, where her masculine dress and sexual advances to women were recorded in the correspondence of numerous of her contemporaries ... but she was accorded all the privileges and honors society believed due a woman of her exalted birth."[89] In

other words, rich women had certain eccentricities tolerated. This proved true later in the mid-twentieth century when First Lady Eleanor Roosevelt maintained a romantic relationship with her own female companion, Lorena Hickok. (See biographies of Roosevelt by Blanche Wiesen Cook.)

[89] Lillian Faderman, *Surpassing the Love of Men*. New York: William Morrow, 1981; p. 55.

Leslie Feinberg, author of *Stone Butch Blues,* offers a thorough history of trans women in *Transgender Warriors,* comparing the more tolerant acceptance of two-spirit individuals in some Native American tribes with the Western heritage of violence against androgynous persons (Joan of Arc was burned as a heretic for cross-dressing; witches were feared in part for their supposed ability to change their sex at will). There are any number of historical accounts of women who dressed as men to gain adventure, disguise themselves against attack, get better wages, etc., but this did not necessarily translate into a sexual preference.

By the 1880s, medical and psychological research on human sexuality began to be taken seriously as a science, but its investigators were European men trained with the sex biases of their time: Sigmund Freud, Havelock Ellis, Magnus Hirschfeld, Richard von Krafft-Ebing. Though sympathetic to bisexual and homosexual identities, Freud set standards for "normalcy" that would affect women (and therapy) for over one hundred years, insisting that an adult female had to accept being dominated and penetrated by a male in order to attain maturity and fulfillment. Any other ambitions or desire for creative alternatives in bed could be written off as *penis envy.* In the midst of a very repressive Victorian era, such frank discussion of human sexual nature led to a backlash against Jewish intellectuals like Freud, and nowhere is that backlash clearer than in Nazi Germany. In Europe, the slender era between the two World Wars saw an explosion of gay and lesbian publishing; lesbian salons in Paris attracting artists and writers from Gertrude Stein to Natalie Barney and Romaine Brooks; nightclubs, performances, and—in Berlin—almost sixty lesbian bars. But Hitler made part of his agenda the total eradication of homosexuals and "decadent art" (though some of his closest advisors were gay male Fascists). Early in the Holocaust, gay and Jewish historian Magnus Hirschfeld had his painstakingly collected library of sex research—over 10,000 volumes—burned to the ground by vindictive Nazis. Who knows how much information on lesbian history was destroyed that night?

What we think of as the *gay and lesbian rights* movement came slowly. Long threatened with reform school, prison, commitment to mental institutions, loss of child custody, and very real threats of bodily harm by police, World War II–era lesbians found one another in the upheaval of wartime, which suddenly encouraged "nice" girls into formerly male roles (the military, industrial war work, baseball) and allowed almost every male privilege from pants to weapons training to athletic strengthening. *Coming Out Under Fire* is a good guide to the wartime changes in self-awareness. But such breakthroughs were temporary, followed by the Cold War backlash and baby boom of the 1950s, when homosexuality was associated with disloyalty to one's country (a strange thing, considering the huge number of gay and lesbian veterans). And, as Faderman points out in her book *To Believe in Women: What Lesbians Have Done For America,* even the anthem "America the Beautiful" was written by a lesbian—Katharine Lee Bates, who wrote to her female partner of 30 years, "I want to love you so much better than I have ever loved."[90]

In 1955, the first lesbian organization in the United States, the Daughters of Bilitis, was organized by Del Martin and Phyllis Lyon—a couple whose enduring love saw them through the rise of civil rights activism in the 1960s, the second wave of feminism's initial hostility to lesbians in the women's movement, the gay liberation awakening after the Stonewall Riots of June 1969, and the rise of lesbian feminist culture in the 1970s, with its music festivals, artwork, film, and bookstores. Phyllis has lived to see an out lesbian prime minister leading a democratic country: Iceland's Johanna Sigurdardottir. At this same moment in history, however, being "caught" as a lesbian in 2011 remains punishable by prison, 100 lashes, rape, or death in countries including Iran, Malaysia, Morocco, Nigeria, Uganda, Zimbabwe …

---

[90] Faderman, *To Believe in Women,* pp. 192–3.

149

Ten good sources for further reading: Bernadette Brooten, *Love Between Women: Early Christian Responses to Female Homoeroticism;* Judith Brown, *Immodest Acts: The Life of a Lesbian Nun in Renaissance Italy;* Lillian Faderman, *Surpassing the Love of Men,* and *Odd Girls and Twilight Lovers;* Leslie Feinberg, *Transgender Warriors;* Sheila Jeffreys, *The Spinster and Her Enemies;* Stephen Murray and Will Roscoe, *Boy Wives and Female Husbands: Studies in African Homosexualities;* Mary Odem, *Delinquent Daughters;* Carroll Smith-Rosenberg, *Disorderly Conduct;* Ruth Vanita and Saleem Kidwai, *Same-Sex Love in India: Readings in History and Literature.*

Looking at the History of Feminism

How do we gather women together, across religious, racial, and class barriers? In light of the countless differences presented here, any alliances seem like a miracle of trust and effort. We know that in American history alone, women striving to organize for their

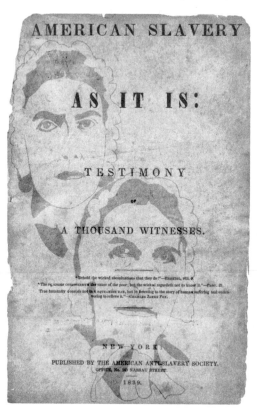

own rights have always been discouraged with some negative label: called, amongst a litany of other names across time, sinful, masculine, unnatural, hysterical, race-traitor, unattractive, socialist, Communist, man-hating, pinko, lesbo, unpatriotic, terrorist. It takes a thick skin to withstand such abuse—and this is merely the American version of backlash against feminism. Therefore, to look at the "waves" of feminist activism bringing about change, including the suffrage movement in different countries and the ongoing movements for reproductive rights and abortion, one must also look at *who* seeks to discredit politically active women—and *why*. Is it only men trying to maintain power and status? No. Women also oppose women. What language appears to mock uppity women in each generation? How is that language racialized, adapted to create fear of immigrant women, gay women, poor women? Who were the stoic female leaders in each country who led the specific movements necessary there? Sometimes we find women who were actual sisters: Sarah and Angelina Grimke in the American South, Margaret Sanger and her sister Ethel, Emmeline, and Christabel Pankhurst in England's suffrage movement. And then there is the sisterhood of every woman whose own history changed the world.

Twelve good sources for further reading: Linda Connolly, *The Irish Women's Movement;* Nancy Cott, *The Grounding of Modern Feminism;* Ellen Dubois and Vicki Ruiz, *Unequal Sisters: A Multicultural Reader in U.S. Women's History;* Sara Evans, *Born for Liberty;* Richard Evans, *The Feminists;* Jo Fisher, *Out of the Shadows: Women, Resistance, and the Politics of South America;* Eleanor Flexner, *A Century of Struggle;* Paula Giddings, *When and Where I Enter;* Radha Kumar, *The History of Doing: An Illustrated Account of Movements for Women's Rights and Feminism in India;* Nell McCafferty, *Nell;* Ruth Rosen, *The World Split Open;* Leila Rupp, *Worlds of Women: The Making of an International Women's Movement.*

These are but a few ways a person newly interested in women's history might choose an approach, ever-mindful that scholars working from other perspectives have much to offer, too. Who are those scholars? Rather, who were the women (and a few men) who first took on the task of organizing women's history as a field? The next chapter offers a brief of history of women's history, and peeks into some curricula and controversies inside today's women's history programs.

Chapter Four

Who Turned Women's History Into an Important Field?

In 1969, for instance, sociologist Pauline Bart, then a visiting assistant professor at Berkeley, introduced a new course on women. A prominent male leftist sociologist warned her, "There simply isn't enough to teach." Laura X, whose home was fast turning into a national archive, mobilized her friends to help Bart. A few weeks later the sociologist arrived at his office and there, tacked onto his door, was a list of one thousand women's names, culled from various historical documents.[91]

Ruth Rosen, *The World Split Open*

This chapter examines when and how *women's history* first began to be a recognized field of study in schools and universities. Is women's history the same thing as *women's studies*? Who are some of the key historians and authors who made it their life's work to produce scholarship on women of the past? When and how did educators interested in women's history first meet to present papers, ex-

[91] Ruth Rosen, interview with Laura X, in *The World Split Open*, New York: Viking, 2000; p. 198.

Nefertiti
Pandora
Hypatia
Boudicea
Sojourner Truth
Harriet Tubman
Angela Bloomer
Margaret Sanger
Jane Addams
Queen Liliuokalani
Emma Goldman
Radclyffe Hall
Rosa Parks
Maria Botchkarova
Ilse Koch
Margaret Thatcher
Joan d Arc
Mary Wollestonecraft
Abigail Adams
The Daughters of Liberty
The Spice Girls
Gerder Lerner
Phylis Wheatley
Betsy Ross
Grainne O Maille
Susan King Taylor
Rosa Luxembourg
Billie Jean King
Marie Curie
Mae Jemison
Wu Tsao
Zlata Filipovic
Ruth & Naomi
Jael & Sisera
Anne Hutchinson
Simone de Beavoir
Benazir Bhutto
Hannah Senesh
Lilith
Tlazolteotl
Sally Hemmings
Harriet Beecher Stowe
Australopithecus
Aphorensis (Lucy)
Eve
Sappho
Cleopatra
Hildegard of Bingen
Hrosvitha
Christine de Pizan
Artemisia Gentileschi
Eleanor of Aquitaine

(continued overleaf...)

change ideas, and promote their books? Which historians accepted the challenge of making resources on women available and age-appropriate for younger students? And what about certain outspoken female historians who just don't like the idea of a "women's history," or argue that the concept has been hijacked by radical feminists?

With so much confusion and dissent, it's remarkable that *Women's History Month* even became part of the American cultural calendar.

However, a quick glance around the U.S. mainstream shows us Girls Scouts working to earn the women's history badge; conservative Senator Kay Bailey Hutchinson promoting a women's history book (and also appearing in a documentary called *If Women Ruled the World*); and prep-school boys cramming to get good scores on the AP U.S. History exam, which occasionally asks questions about—women's history!

©GSUSA

In fact, good-quality women's history has become a marketable commodity; and a product one can invest in. There's a National Women's History Museum being planned for the Washington, D.C., mall; Smithsonian exhibits on women at war with "Rosie the Riveter" lunch boxes and key chains available in the museum shop (ironically, manufactured for the United States by female factory workers in China); and graduate programs offering advanced degrees in women's history at colleges and universities around the country. It took a good 40 years of activism to bring about this change.

Until the late 1960s, there wasn't a mainstream market for historical knowledge about women. Important pockets of learning about the contributions of great women existed, for the most part, at elite women's colleges like Bryn Mawr and Smith, founded by

154

women who believed in women.[92] But although in the United States girls as well as boys were required to get an education (provided more or less free through public schooling), American educational standards never required either girls or boys to learn women's history. Nor, until recently, were black or white children exposed to the experiences and contributions of African-Americans and other nonwhites.

Voices of protest against these educational omissions finally began to be heard after the Second World War. The Allied victory had resulted, in part, from the selfless contributions of diverse American citizens: black and white, male and female. In the postwar 1950s, during an ideological war and scientific arms race against the Soviet Union, how could America still claim to be the land of the free when its colleges locked out black and female talent—deliberately disadvantaging more than half of American minds? The cost of discouraging girls from math, science, and engineering careers in America hit home when the first woman in space, Valentina Tereshkova, blasted off from the Soviet Union in 1963. It would take another *20 years* before the U.S. allowed its first female astronaut, Sally Ride, into space.

Civil rights' focus on all children's right to an education—and what *educated Americans* should learn—meant openly challenging the glaring biases, and silences, in both newspapers and standardized schoolbooks. This cause gained support from a new generation of black and white educators empowered by the historic *Brown v. Board of Education* decision in 1954, which directed American schools to desegregate, "with all deliberate speed."

Dedicated to providing authentic materials and documents adaptable to the needs of the times, teachers and writers scrambled to introduce "relevant" materials into gradually integrated, diverse classrooms. First the civil rights movement (1954–74) and then second-wave feminism (1960–80) forced the entire nation to take a hard look at how race and sex discrimination were holding back the achievement of all children in America's schools.

---

[92] Again, see Lillian Faderman's excellent guide, *To Believe in Women,* an overview of the founders of women's colleges and their strong relationship ties.

Legacies of the Civil Rights Era

By the early 1960s, in this climate of civil rights change (and the emergence of obvious role models such as Rosa Parks, Fannie Lou Hamer, and Dr. Martin Luther King Jr.), advocates for teaching black history were demanding changes to the American history curriculum in particular. A powerful argument for more inclusive studies was that adding material on black achievement would engage students in their own heritage, fostering pride rather than resentment and mistrust of authority. Furthermore, because even the brightest black students had been kept out of the country's top private colleges (and, in Southern states, denied access to whites-only public universities and law schools), white students lacked exposure to (and regular interaction with) black artists, inventors, and intellectuals. African-Americans who had succeeded nationally and locally, in spite of segregation and backlash, were missing from the record. *Everyone* needed remedial education about how people of color had contributed to creating the United States as a world power.

What does it mean when your own history does not matter enough to be counted as "real" history; or, worse, is considered too troubling or radical to mention in the course of a school day? Educational psychologists, as well as historians, tackled this question as an important clue for understanding differences in students' test scores, "aptitude"—and attitude. James Loewen later explored these issues in his popular book *Lies My Teacher Told Me*.

The way American history is taught particularly alienates students of color and children from impoverished families. Feel-good history for affluent white males inevitably amounts to feel-bad history for everyone else…. Black students consider American history, as usually taught, "white" and assimilative, so they resist learning it. This explains why research shows a bigger performance differential between

156

poor and rich students, or black and white students, in history than in other school subjects. Girls also dislike social studies and history even more than boys, probably because women and women's concerns and perceptions still go underrepresented in history classes.[93]

These issues were not limited to the United States. Recalling her childhood in Jamaica, Opal Palmer Adisa wrote:

I never thought of myself as a writer, I suppose as a result of being reared in a colonial society with a British education that vociferously denounced Jamaica's cultural ethos. In fact, we were presumed to lack history and therefore had nothing worthwhile to write about. I always suspected this history I was being taught was somehow erroneous or at best lopsided and suspect. I didn't feel wrong or inferior, yet ... I can say with perfect honesty that I never read a book or a poem by a black person, from anywhere in the world, until I was sixteen and had moved to New York.[94]

But there was a catch to the new language of black pride and black power: a clearly masculine emphasis. For so long, white men had denied full adult rights to black men, had lynched them for "looking" at white women, belittled them publicly by calling them "boy." Manhood was now linked to the ideal of full equality and public participation in ways *womanhood* had never symbolized political power in any community. Thus, various photographs of the civil rights era show black men picketing in front of the White House, or marching with Dr. Martin Luther King, while wearing placards that simply state, "I am a man."

One hundred years earlier, freed slave Sojourner Truth had used the slogan "Ain't I a

[93] James Loewen, *Lies My Teacher Told Me.* New York: Touchstone, 1996; pp. 301–302

[94] Opal Palmer Adisa, "Lying in the Tall Grasses, Eating Cane," From *The Eloquent Essay,* ed. John Loughery. New York: Persea Books, 2000, pp. 185–86; originally published in *ZYZZYVA,* 1998.

woman?" to provoke similar consciousness-raising among whites; her famous speech pointed out the infinite ways Southern chivalry toward women's delicacy was never extended to hard-laboring *black* women. Her words simply can't be quoted enough: "That man over there says that women need to be helped into carriages, and lifted over ditches, and to have the best place everywhere. Nobody ever helps me into carriages, or over mud-puddles, or gives me any best place! And ain't I a woman?" But in the new push for *human* rights in the 1960s, most campaigns for change featured men as the focus. It was still normal for women of any group to have fewer rights than men, and, as a result, more shocking when men were discriminated against in a nation built around the slogan "all *men* are created equal." Americans determined to create social change—peacefully—kept their emphasis on ideals of brotherhood, the dignity of every man, and similar male-identified rhetoric. Even that hyper-feminine icon of the early 1960s, Marilyn Monroe, used this language in a plea for racial tolerance, unaware of the irony as she declared in one interview, "We are all brothers."

Where were women in these narratives of freedom? To be sure, many were right out front in the civil rights movement—whether in song and organizing (Bernice Johnson Reagon, Ruby Doris Smith, Cynthia Washington), in politics (Ella Baker, Fannie Lou Hamer), in radical action (Angela Davis). Black women also had the options of embodying new and different female representations, ranging from veiled Black Muslim to armed Black Panther, making clear their distinction from white women and mainstream white women's issues. Coretta Scott King and Malcolm X's widow Betty Shabazz rivaled Jackie Kennedy as grieving but dignified wives in a decade sadly defined by multiple political assassinations. In contrast, the *women's liberation movement* emerging simultaneously during the

1960s was portrayed by the media (when it covered feminism at all) as a primarily white, middle-class cohort of women who came from privileged socioeconomic backgrounds.

And then there was the looming background of the Vietnam War. Reporters haggard from covering the death toll of America's best young men wondered why suburban white women, who had no draft to fear, were marching for *more* rights while young men feared for their lives in South Asian jungles. (The notion that the Vietnam War directly affected the women and girls of Vietnam, or that American servicewomen posted as military nurses also returned with post traumatic distress disorder, was rarely acknowledged.) Women's history wasn't a priority for most journalists looking for a blood-and-guts story to file. Between cartoonish stereotypes of whiny white women and armed black women—trivial reductions easily manipulated by conservatives looking to restore order—a united American sisterhood seemed impossible.

But women who participated in the civil rights movement—whether black, white, Jewish, or Latina—were rapidly gaining a sophisticated political education. The New Left was saturated with dialogue and literature on how the minds, bodies, and imaginations of the oppressed can become colonized. Soon women were observing similarities between the cultural repression of racial *minorities* and their own invisibility when *gender* was taken into account. However, while minority women certainly desired greater empowerment for themselves, they were also keenly sensitive to their alliances with men of color. Black men and women shared the overarching experience of white harassment, and there was additional pressure on black women not to air the dirty laundry of private, personal abuses by the men of their own ethnic communities. White feminists were insisting that *the personal is political*—a slogan contributed by Carol Hanisch, who had done civil rights work in rural Mississippi in the mid-1960s.[95] But black women in the civil rights movement did not necessarily trust white feminists to have all the answers, perceiving a lack of consciousness on racial hierarchies when feminist narratives lumped

---

[95] Ruth Rosen, *The World Split Open*, p. 196.

all men together. Finally, many women of color did not see their specific issues of work, housing, and family being addressed by white feminist theories developing at the time.

Soon enough, an exciting cadre of black feminist scholars and authors would give voice to perspectives by women of color, launching bold works by writers such as Michele Wallace, bell hooks, Paula Giddings, Patricia Hill Collins, Mary Frances Berry, Alice Walker, and Audre Lorde. The explosion of protest at ways scholarship on black women's history had been ignored culminated in the powerful volume *All the Women Are White, All the Blacks Are Men, But Some of Us Are Brave,* edited by Gloria T. Hull, Patricia Bell Scott, and Barbara Smith. Not published until 1982 (by the Feminist Press established by Florence Howe), it brought together the best of current research on black women's history and literature, including valuable bibliographies and source lists, and such chapter titles as "Afro-American Women, 1800–1910: A Selected Bibliography" (Jean Fagan Yellin); "Racism and Women's Studies" (Barbara Smith); "Studying Slavery: Some Literary and Pedagogical Considerations" (Erlene Stetson); and "Doing the Work: Selected Course Syllabi." A celebratory follow-up volume, *Still Brave,* was launched by the Feminist Press in 2009, edited by Stanlie M. James, Frances Smith Foster and Beverly Guy-Sheftall. But it would take years before concepts like *intersectionality* encouraged women's history scholars and activists to look at the ways multiple identities—and interlocking systems of bias—affected women's lives. Although the late 1960s and early 1970s offered a terribly exciting climate of action, women slow to take on the hard work of *building alliances* lost important ground by excluding (or turning on) one another. Mainstream feminist groups such as NOW (the National Organization for Women) and the staff of *Ms.* magazine had mostly white leadership, and struggled with the perspectives/inclusion of openly lesbian women as well.

Just at the moment when *women's history* began to be rediscovered, celebrated, and published in books, posters and calendars, an undercurrent of conflict at conferences and workshops revealed the impossibility of pretending that all women shared a heritage or an easy sisterhood. These tensions were especially apparent at the global UN conferences on women staged in Mexico City in 1975, Copenhagen in 1980, and Nairobi in 1985. Any historical discussion would have to include basic realities: women had *owned* women in U.S. history. Some women still expected their female "help" to come and go by the back door, even as they held women's club meetings in the front room. Betty Friedan had declared any membership of lesbians in NOW to be a "lavender menace." Plenty of lesbian bars still turned away black patrons. Plenty of women's colleges had rejected Jews.

Nonetheless, too many women had tirelessly advocated for men's civil rights, and were growing disgusted that so few men were now willing to advocate for women's rights. Activist women who did raise "the woman question" within radical organizations found they were patronized, jeered, silenced, or ignored. Even in the 1960s' exciting climate of social change, demands for broader participation by women met with resistance from the male leaders of liberation movements. Radical men, it turned out, were often quite traditional on the subject of women. It was *men's* freedom from humiliation by other men which characterized freedom-fighting. Women's support of men was very much welcome. But few revolutionary men saw women's issues as a cause equal to their own oppression by tyrants or colonial powers. To grant women the status of *humans,* making *women's rights* inseparable from *human rights,* would cost oppressed men what little power they already enjoyed: the power to be master in the home, the family, the marriage.

In the introduction to her book on women in the American Revolution, historian Linda Kerber wrote, "Even the most radical American men had not intended to make a revolution in the status of their wives and sisters."[96] Kerber found that colonial women taking part in Revolutionary activities were sadly aware they could expect little change for their own status; one woman, Mary Livingston, wrote in October 1776, "You know that our Sex are *doomed* to be obedient in every stage of life so that we shant be great gainers by this contest."[97] Why had the ideals of the Enlight-

---

[96] Linda Kerber, *Women of the Republic.* W.W. Norton, 1986; p. 9.

[97] Ibid., p. 35; from the Ridley Papers, Massachusetts Historical Society, Boston.

enment failed to free women, as well as men? Kerber's grim reminder: "Even Rousseau, one of the most radical political theorists of an age famous for its ability to examine inherited assumptions, failed to examine his own assumptions about women. Ought a woman dare to think?"[98]

This tension appears over and over in history, and is also a part of our national heritage; almost every great male leader has balked at the question of adding women's rights to new male freedoms. A sampling:

1776: Abigail Adams complains to John, "I can not say I think you very generous to the Ladies, for whilst you are proclaiming peace and good will to Men, Emancipating all Nations, you insist upon retaining an absolute power over Wives … and notwithstanding all your wise Laws and Maxims we have it in our power not only to free ourselves but to subdue our Masters."

1838: Theodore Weld warns Sarah Grimke "not to push your women's rights until human rights have gone ahead."

1870: Frederick Douglass tells white suffragists, upset that the new Fifteenth Amendment grants voting rights to black men but not to any women, "To you the vote is desirable; to us it is necessary."

1970: Robin Morgan's groundbreaking anthology *Sisterhood is Powerful* begins with "A Sampling of Sexist Quotes" by radical men, such as, "The only position for women in SNCC is prone" (Stokeley Carmichael); and "The only alliance I would make with the women's movement is in bed" (Abbie Hoffman).[99]

In assembling a litany of such quotes, Morgan wrote candidly about why so many politically-minded men refused to acknowl-

---

[98] Ibid., p. 27.

[99] Robin Morgan, ed., *Sisterhood is Powerful*. New York: Random House, 1970; pp. 37–38. For a fair and thorough discussion of the events leading to Carmichael's remarks after women presented a critique of sex discrimination in the Student Nonviolent Coordinating Committee, see Ruth Rosen, *The World Split Open*, pp. 105–110.

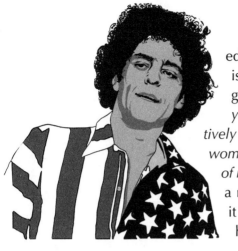

"The only alliance I would make with the Women's Movement is in bed..."
Abbie Hoffman.

edge systematic sexism as an issue affecting women in struggle. *"How, we are asked, can you talk about the comparatively insignificant oppression of women, when set beside the issues of racism and imperialism?* This is a male-supremacist question ... it dares to weigh and compute human suffering, and it places oppressed groups in competition with each other (an old and very capitalistic trick: divide and conquer)."[100] In communities with limited resources, this argument about prioritizing action raged for decades; a debate of theory, as well as action. Which issue came first, racism or sexism? Without tackling racism, women of all colors would never unite. But without confronting sexism in society, fewer girls would reach adulthood alive—or become educated enough to speak up on any issue.

Women of color, of course, remained caught in the middle, fending off mistaken assumptions that anyone could "choose" between race and gender identity, yet expected to build coalitions with feminist initiatives led by white women. (Paying tribute to Congresswoman Shirley Chisholm, who ran for President in 1972, D.C. Congresswoman Eleanor Holmes Norton recalled, *"She* began with the coalition between her black self and her female self.") And all of this affected who emerged as the face of women's history scholarship in America. From the very beginning, women's history advocates were forced to clarify their alliances. Would they be historians, first—or feminists? Educators—or activists? Would women's history address the contributions of black women, and acknowledge their struggles, or merely perpetuate the usual emphasis on achievement by white people? Attaining credibility, either in academic or progressive circles, depended mightily on how

---

[100] Ibid., p. xxxix

a scholar of women's history identified her loyalties.

By the late 1960s, campus sit-ins and protests had grown to include student demands for courses that genuinely reflected current social issues. Both *women's studies* and *black studies* programs were being added to colleges around the country, though not without backlash. These important new fields attracted different advocates and constituents—reflecting ongoing debate over ranking oppressions and identities. Where should a university appoint its first black feminist scholar?—In the women's studies program, or in the hardwon Black Studies Department? Did a black woman have to specialize in black women?[101] Why was she assumed to be interested, or expert, in the history of slavery or the history of women's suffrage—couldn't she teach Russian history, for heaven's sake, if that was in fact her doctoral specialty? And that begged the larger question of how women's history in general should be integrated into Western civilization courses—which were at that time primarily taught by men, with male graduate assistants. Should only women be hired to teach women's history? Could classes ever be allowed to enroll *women only,* like those which theologian Mary Daly dared to teach at Boston College? Wasn't a total emphasis on women just reverse discrimination? And how could anyone be expected to be able

---

[101] See Barbara Christian's essay, "But Who Do You Really Belong To—Black Studies or Women's Studies?" first published in 1989. In *Still Brave: The Evolution of Black Women's Studies,* ed. Stanlie James, Frances Smith Foster and Beverly Guy-Sheftall. New York: The Feminist Press, 2009; pp. 86–91.

[102] In some institutions, opportunities to teach innovative new courses were reserved for the most senior faculty as a matter of privilege, not preparation. At one university where I taught, the new women's history course was "given" to the most senior female professor, who had little background in the subject matter and was not interested in teaching it, whereas I had just completed a doctorate in women's history but had low ranking as the most recently hired member of the faculty.

to teach this material, when the subject had never been taught?[102]

An entire new field was about to be born. Where *women's studies* seemed destined for a radical reputation, rooted in activism and critique of patriarchy, the new possibility of examining women's lives as subject matter appealed to scholars who were already committed to academic careers in the history discipline. Against this background of divergent approaches to feminism, a core group of young and mid-career female professors, most of whom taught in New York, New England, and California, were determined to produce the quality scholarship that would put women's history on an equal footing with any course offered at any college. They would go on to create "a canon of their own," textbooks that withstood the test of time as invaluable additions (or rivals) to the standard male-only surveys then taught to history majors. The very titles of these new works expressed how much history had been left out—and how much important material there was, now, to learn: *Becoming Visible. Hidden From History. A Heritage of Her Own. Women Have Always Worked. When God Was a Woman. A Century of Struggle. We Were There. One Half the People. Liberating Women's History. Moving the Mountain. Born*

for Liberty. The Creation of Patriarchy.

The Groundbreakers

Because educators in a position to make hiring decisions were usually tenured white males, women applying to teach at coed institutions competed against each other for the sole "token female" openings in history departments. And not all were eager to be brought into academia under the banner of being a *feminist* historian, a label some found limiting (and others embraced, but privately felt might hold back professional advancement). The solution to serious employment often lay in single-sex women's colleges. Some were religious in affiliation, yet remarkably open to offering new courses on the women's movement, and saw nothing strange in hiring qualified female scholars as role models for young women. This meant that a small Catholic campus like Notre Dame College in Manchester, New Hampshire, had nuns teaching "History of Women" and a science course called "The Female Body" in 1973, while just a few miles away, the tiny Ivy League Dartmouth College had yet to enroll any female bodies at all. The elite Seven Sisters colleges—Barnard, Bryn Mawr, Mount Holyoke, Radcliffe, Smith, Vassar, and Wellesley—of course had been founded in the nineteenth century with the goal of offering young women an education equivalent to that available to their brothers; they had a tradition of female leadership—and a very exclusive student body. Other "arts" colleges for women, such as Sarah Lawrence and Bennington, permitted female scholars greater range for innovation. Thus at first one found historian Gerda Lerner

teaching at Sarah Lawrence; Nancy Cott teaching at Wellesley; and Alice Rossi teaching at Goucher College in Maryland.

On the other hand, private and Catholic single-sex colleges were not only prohibitively expensive; they could also be unwelcoming to black and Jewish students. Fortunately, Jewish and minority women undergraduates were soon enrolling in city and state colleges and night schools with excellent women's history curricula. In 1971, one might study with Renate Bridenthal at Brooklyn College; with Rosalyn Baxandall at Queens College; or just take a history course on "Women and the Law" from a quiet, brainy professor named Ruth Bader Ginsburg, then teaching at Rutgers University–Newark and decades away from being appointed as the second female justice on the U.S. Supreme Court.

By the turn of the 1970s most universities offered at least one course with a neutral-sounding title such as "Women in American History." During the 1971–72 academic year, for example, undergraduate students could enroll in a basic women's history course at schools as different as Arkansas College, Brown University, Columbia University, the Detroit Institute of the Arts, the University of Georgia, the University of Iowa, the University of Notre Dame in Indiana, the New School for Social Research, St. Peter's College of Jersey City, Texas Tech, Vassar, and the University of Vermont.[103] And they would be learning from other women who set the gold standard in women's history research and publishing: Johnetta Cole, Linda Gordon, Alice Kessler-Harris, Mary Lefkowitz, Sarah Pomeroy, Hilda Smith, Carroll Smith-Rosenberg, and Anne Firor Scott.

Who were these women? As their names suggest, an impressive number were Jewish immigrants, including Holocaust survivors or refugees whose personal histories had well-acquainted them with the perspective of an outsider. Some were, in fact, turning the lens of gender toward greater understanding of German history (Claudia Koontz). Others immersed in the current debate over women's health and reproductive rights were producing research on how medical authorities had controlled women's choices for centuries

---

[103] Source: *Who's Who and Where in Women's Studies*. New York: The Feminist Press, 1974.

(Judith Walker Leavitt, Susan Reverby, Carole Vance). A few bold women were applying scholarly methods to producing new histories of lesbian identity in the past (Carroll Smith-Rosenberg, Lillian Faderman). Other women had been faculty wives, sacrificing scholarly advancement for the career good of their husbands, while experiencing critical backlash within academia for their own ambitions. And many had been inspired by the influences of second-wave feminism to return to academic work, seeing with new eyes how slowly women attained promotion, grants, office space, research support, or tenure. Alice Rossi, who edited the enormously popular women's history collection *The Feminist Papers* (first published in 1973 and still in use), wrote of her own academic journey in the 1972 volume entitled *The American Sisterhood*.

As a faculty wife ... I saw numerous instances of women being kept off the academic turf their husbands claimed as their own.... I watched women friends leave the university when they became pregnant and being kept out when they tried to return after their children entered school.... It took a return to academia, involving a traumatic encounter with the discrimination women so often suffer, to jar me out of my innocence.

> My own concern for the status of women, the analysis of sex roles, the study of and active participation in abortion law and divorce reform, I date to the "slow burn" that began in that first major encounter with sex discrimination in academia.[104]

After Rossi published her first scholarly paper on women and sex equality, her husband actually "...received a sympathetic bereavement cased from a West Coast sociologist for having such an upstart wife."[105]

Florence Howe, who also contributed an essay to *The American Sisterhood,* wrote of the limited climate she observed for academic women throughout the 1960s; having young women attend college was not the same thing as encouraging their success in graduate degree work.

---

[104] Alice Rossi, "Women—Terms of Liberation, 1970." In Wendy Martin, ed., *The American Sisterhood.* New York: Harper & Row, 1972; pp. 130–31.

[105] Ibid., p. 131.

Even in 1969, it is assumed that women who go to college are generally sitting out four years of their lives before becoming wives and mothers. During my nine years at Goucher, I have found little encouragement for any other view. Unfortunately, statistics bear me out only too well ... there are fewer women on the faculties of women's colleges than there were in the 30s; the percentage of women on the faculty of the University of Chicago has dropped from 8 per cent at the end of the nineteenth century to a recent low of 2 per cent....[106]

Gerda Lerner created a permanent name of honor in the women's history field by avoiding a focus on women's oppression—but documenting it simultaneously. Although blunt in naming the parentheses of women's lives—two of her best texts are the two-volume series entitled *The Creation of Patriarchy* and *The Creation of Feminist Consciousness*—Lerner demanded that her students and readers ask, "What did these women need to be to achieve in their own era?" Using phrases such as "authorization through motherhood," Lerner looked at what women did within their permitted spheres. In her own words:

I have in my own work learned that it is far more useful to deal with the question of victimization as one aspect of women's history, but never to regard it as the central aspect of women's history. Essentially, treating women as victims of oppression once again places them in a male-defined conceptual framework: oppressed, victimized by standards and values established by men. The true story of women is the history of their ongoing functioning in that male-defined world, on their own terms.[107]

In 1981, while serving as president of the OAH (the Organization of American Historians), Lerner created the distinguished Lectureship Program on women's history, bringing together a roster

[106] Florence Howe, "The Education of Women, 1970," in *The American Sisterhood,* ibid. p. 272.

[107] Gerda Lerner, "Placing Women in History: A 1975 Perspective." In *Liberating Women's History,* ed. Berenice Carroll. University of Chicago Press, 1976; pp. 358-59.

of female scholars who had specialized in the study of U.S. women; today this resource includes over one hundred exceptional professors and writers.

Kathyrn Kish Sklar, who with her spouse Thomas Dublin built a women's history program first at UCLA and then at SUNY Binghamton in upstate New York, focused on nineteenth-century women's work in her award-winning book *Catharine Beecher: A Study in American Domesticity*. This approach required that students of women's history look beyond the usual suffrage heroines. Beecher, rather than embracing political feminism, elevated traditional women's work to a serious sceince. Alice Kessler-Harris, whose books included *Out to Work* and *Women Have Always Worked*, emphasized the issues of gender and labor history, directing students to understand that women had not simply

started having careers in the 1970s. All the women in what might be called the first generation of women's history programs brought exacting standards to the graduate programs they developed and the next generation of students they helped train.

The Berks

By the 1970s, there were enough women's history professors, students, and affiliated research centers to support national conferences on the subject of women's history. Women were increasingly outspoken about the inclusion of their work in mainstream organizations such as the OAH (Organization of American

Historians) and the AHA (the American History Association). Some scholars organized subcommittees, such as the CCWHP (Coordinating Committee for Women in the History Profession), which held lunch and breakfast sessions during the AHA annual meeting. But there was also a membership called the Berkshire Conference of Women Historians, which produced an event called the Berkshire Conference on the History of Women (fondly nicknamed "the Berks" by those involved). As noted in the program of their eighth conference:

A group of about twenty historians on the faculties of several women's colleges in New England and New York first met on a spring weekend at an inn in the Connecticut countryside in 1930 and constituted themselves the Lakeville History Group.... About 1935 the name Berkshire Historical Conference was adopted to reflect the location where meetings were usually held. It was incorporated in 1981.... Since 1972 the Berkshire Conference of Women Historians has awarded prizes for historical writing by women.

berkshire conference
OF **WOMEN HISTORIANS**

First held in 1973 at Douglass College, and meeting every few years thereafter on the lush campuses of historic women's colleges such as Smith, Vassar, and Wellesley, the Berks brought together hundreds of interested women (and men) to hear scholarly papers, interview for teaching positions, and find graduate mentors. Who wouldn't enjoy a chance to mingle with the most impressive names in women's history scholarship? At the sixth Berks, for instance, held at Smith College in June 1984, it was possible to hear speeches and papers presented by Gerda Lerner, Mary Beth Norton, Elizabeth Fox-Genovese, Nancy Cott, Zillah Eisenstein, Mary Frances Berry, Louise Tilly, Joan Jacobs Brumberg—and then mingle with these illustrious scholars during a full complement of cocktail receptions, dinners, poetry readings, and a gallery exhibit on Elizabeth Cady Stanton and Susan B. Anthony at the Sophia Smith collection. Additional evening activities offered cultural tributes to female composers, filmmakers, playwrights, musicians, authors, and oral historians. Any student who had borne the frustration and shame of being told by a college advisor, "There just isn't enough material to do a thesis on women's history," returned from the Berks absolutely saturated with primary materials, colleagues, and tools for starting database research (such valuable information had to be hunted down individually in those the pre-internet days; computer searches and even email were not routinely available to most historians until the early 1990s). Arriving at my first Berkshire Conference in June 1984 as a 23-year-old graduate student just completing my first year of work in a demanding Ph.D. program, I felt like the proverbial kid in a candy store—or the prospecting miner who has just tumbled into the Mother Lode of gold.

As time went on, more male graduate students and faculty began participating in the Berks, a healthy indication of the growing popularity of women's history as a research field.

Here are some sample session titles from the programs of past Berkshire Conference meetings. The range of topics is a good illustration of how women's history, like men's, must be approached in terms of region, ethnicity, class, race, and time frame.

Wives and Widows in Medieval England

Female Textile Workers in the South

Right Wing Women in France and Germany in the 1920s

Women's History in Scandinavia

Women's Prison History: Issues of Sex and Race

Publishing Women's History: A Roundtable Discussion (with agents and editors)

Gender and Space in Revolutionary Paris

Women's Poverty in Eighteenth-Century London

Video Testimonies of Women Survivors of the Holocaust

Royal Women in the Ancient World

Lesbian Bar Communities of the 1940s and 50s

Sex and Marriage in Colonial Mexico

Integrating U.S. Women's History into the Secondary-School Curriculum

Women's Archives, Women Archivists

Transvestism as Transgression, 1880-1980

Empire and the Woman Question in India and Jamaica

Gender and the History of Early Modern Medicine

These events often were the first opportunity for a young graduate student to present new work, creating a link between her original research and the scholars who went before her. As the years passed, challenges and controversies also became part of the semiannual conference—demands for more lesbian history, larger T-shirt sizes, better child care, vegan food, and perhaps most wrenchingly, dissent over whether historians should testify in the 1986 *Sears v. EOCC* court case (see p 177). But with several generations in the same space, each observing the burgeoning of interest in women as a subject, happy tears and raised fists characterized the celebratory mood over concluding toasts to collective success and progress.

Do You Have to Be a Feminist to Teach Women's History?

The field of women's history attracted scholars of every political stripe and research interest. In this way it is no different from *men's* history: We don't assume that, say, a student interested in the life of Mozart is aligned with any particular political movement—we assume he's probably interested in Mozart. However, women interested in women's history did confront assumptions that they were *only* motivated by a feminist impulse to reclaim important, overlooked women; this discussion dominated an interesting anthology called *Liberating Women's History: Theoretical and Critical Essays,* published in 1976. Without question, the women's history field emerged against a backdrop of feminist activism in the 1970s, at a time when other women faculty were launching charges of sexist bias in education. It was almost impossible to dodge the question, "Are you some kind of feminist?" For bright women, the doors of academia might be held open wider, but the field of women's history was seen as a dead-end proposition.

"Why study women? That won't get you anywhere" is a remark I reflect on at length in my own teaching memoir, *Revenge of the Women's Studies Professor.* As late as 1983, when I was accepted into a graduate program in women's history, one close friend described my career as "majoring in women's lib," where my male colleagues embarking on dissertations about men in history were not perceived as acting on allegiances to "men's lib." (If anything, early American history could rightly be called "American lib.")

Hard-working professors and independent scholars resented being called 'radical' just because they mentioned the existence of women. A few elected to release strong statements, carefully distancing their work from feminism. Aileen Kraditor is a good example. Her brilliant work, *Ideas of the Woman Suffrage Movement,* is one of the best histories available on how American women won the vote. In her 1979 "Preface to the Norton Edition," Kraditor declared:

> I [did not] choose this topic as a contribution to a cause. I did not then, nor do I now, think that any aspect of women's history is "what is important to know about women" more than any other, or that a scholar's choice of topics should be guided by didactic motives.... Among the changes I would not make would be to replace "chairman" and "spokesmen" by "chairperson," or "chair," and "spokeswomen," which seem to me barbarisms.... Unfortunately, a large proportion of the recent literature on women's history has been motivated more by the desire to provide current feminists with a heritage of oppression-plus-achievement than by the desire to find out what happened. It is, consequently, often of poor quality.[108]

As the field of women's history gained credibility during the 1980s, after the election of President Reagan, the United States was also witnessing a considerable backlash against the gains of the women's movement (and the emergent gay rights movement as well). Dismissive critiques of gender studies/women's studies led some scholars to renounce women's history practices, or to ex-

---

[108] Aileen Kraditor, *Ideas of the Woman Suffrage Movement, 1890–1920.* W.W. Norton, 1981; pp. v–viii.

pose what they perceived as failings in the discipline. During the 1990s, academic women as varied as Camille Paglia, Elizabeth Fox-Genovese, Jean Bethke Elshtain, Mary Lefkowitz, Gertrude Himmelfarb, and Daphne Patai wrote critically of what they contended were faulty feminist standpoints or politicized climates in academic programs. Some women joined conservative organizations intended to investigate, expose, and refute what they believed were liberal biases in academia: organizations such as the National Association of Scholars, Accuracy in Academia, the Women's Freedom Network, and the Independent Women's Forum.[109] Opposition to women's increasing participation in military leadership became the personal campaign of Elaine Donnelly, whose Center for Military Readiness also opposed any relaxation of the bans on gays serving openly in the armed forces; politically high-ranked women including Linda Chavez and Lynne Cheney criticized multiculturalism in higher education; Jessica Gavora, who became a speechwriter for Attorney General John Ashcroft, attacked the increasing opportunities for girls in sports in her book *Tilting the Playing Field;* and one of Christina Hoff Sommers' book titles charged that the focus on how sexism in schools held back girls was really *The War Against Boys.* (Of course, women had appeared on opposing sides of heated discussions *about women* since long before the first wave of feminism. In the nineteenth century, American women were famously divided by the ideals of the Civil War, the temperance movement, the birth-control movement, justice for immigrant and minority women, labor, and much more—including the vote. Consider the many white Southern women whose loyalty to the Confederate cause included strongly defending the enslavement of black women.)

During the 1970s, Phyllis Schlafly's Stop ERA campaign became an infamous example of one woman's national crusade to defeat the Equal Rights Amendment; Schlafly's *The Power of the Positive Woman* and Marabel Morgan's *Total Woman* were book titles calculated to portray "women's libbers" as negative—and less than fully feminine. Neoconservatives such as Midge Decter emerged to write theory crit-

---

[109] See Elayne Rapping, "The Ladies Who Lynch," in *On the Issues,* spring 1996; pp. 7–9.

176

ical of feminist goals, paving the way for an entire wave of conservative women activists—familiar and very powerful figures today.

One ironic shift seen in the 1980s and 90s was that feminists' push for social reform helped antifeminist women gain access to graduate school, law school, and the media. This new generation of well-credentialed conservative women with strong media skills would soon be available to evangelical think tanks, family-values institutions, and even mainstream corporations looking for ways to argue against raising women's wages. But women who identified wholeheartedly as feminists, too, could face off against one another; in the language of second-wave feminism, this was often referred to as "trashing." (The less respectful term "catfight," when used by men to depict the spectacle of women in conflict, had both erotic and belittling overtones.)

Where women's history scholars were in disagreement about the lessons of history, however, the stakes were high. In one dramatic trial taking place during the mid-1980s, *Sears v. EEOC,* the opposing sides each retained women's history professors as expert witnesses on the history of women and work. The division ripped through the women's history profession, resulting in a wave of symposia and articles.[110]

The Sears trial concerned female employees who charged that the Sears company systematically paid women less—and put them in jobs where they earned lower commissions and had less likelihood of promotion. The Equal Employment Opportunity Commission (EEOC) filed suit against Sears in 1979; the case did not go to trial until 1984. By then, Sears had prepared a counterargument: that women themselves entered the hiring process with a preference for part-time jobs, and that women's difference from men led them to assignments in certain departments where commission pay and advancement also happened to be different.

Lawyers for Sears presented feminist historian Rosalind Rosenberg to testify about women's occupational history, and Rosenberg suggested that men and women were in fact motivated by different

---

[110] See *Washington Post* editorial, June 9, 1986; *Ms.* magazine (July 1986), *Signs 11* (1986), *Feminist Studies 12* (1986), *Feminist Review 25* (1987), *Texas Law Review* (December 1988).

approaches to the labor market—women being more likely to accept part-time labor which meshed with their child care responsibilities. "Historically, men and women have had different interests, goals, and aspirations regarding work…. Even today, many women choose jobs that complement their family obligations over jobs that might increase and enhance their earning potential."[111] (Sears had also solicited the testimony of historian Kathryn Kish Sklar, who told them she would not testify against equal employment.)

The EEOC then recruited my own professor, historian Alice Kessler-Harris, who testified on the legacies of a segregated labor force rooted in biased assumptions about which jobs were appropriate for women. "The question is, how is inequality *best* explained?" She said. "Rosalind Rosenberg says by women's 'differences,' by the choices women make. I suggest discrimination."[112] Throughout 1985 and 1986, the women's history profession exploded with controversy, many circulating multiple letters condemning Rosenberg, although a critical minority defended her choice to interpret women's history any way she saw fit. In December 1985, at the annual meeting of the American Historical Association, the Coordinating Committee of Women in the Historical Profession passed a strongly worded resolution declaring, "As feminist scholars we have a responsibility not to allow our scholarship to be used against the interests of women struggling or equity in our society."[113] Ultimately, the court sided with Sears, and the EEOC lost their case. But the mood created by this academic showdown disturbed even the famously liberal *Washington Post,* which published an editorial asserting, "It's fine to attack Professor Rosenberg's position on the Sears case, the quality of her research or the use she put it to. But to argue that she should not, regardless of her beliefs, testify 'against women's interests' is to apply, blindly, a party line." These issues would arise over and over: How and when should experts on women's history use that expertise to serve the interests of living women?

---

[111] Carol Sternhell, "What Happens When Feminists Turn Up on Both Sides of the Courtroom?" In *Ms.,* July 1986; p. 50.

[112] Ibid., p. 51.

National Women's History Month and the National Women's History Project

While political issues at the graduate level women's history re-search were being debated in the mid-eighties, one woman was making it her mission to bring basic women's history into every-day lives and schools. Starting with a simple Women's History Week in her own county in 1978, she eventually helped inaugurate National Women's History Month. Her name: Molly Murphy MacGregor.

MacGregor cofounded the National Women's History Project, or NWMP, in 1980, along with Mary Ruthsdotter, Marai Cuevas, Paula Hammett, and Bette Morgan, ultimately producing a catalogue of materials teachers could order from in order to access secondary-school materials for lesson plans on women. According to the NWHP website:

> In 1980, we were a group of women who noticed that women were absent from our texts. Mo more than 3 per-cent of the content was devoted to women....
> We convinced Congress and the White House of the need for our nation to celebrate and recognize women's role in history on an annual basis. As a result of our efforts, the week of March 8th (International Women's Day) was officially designated as National Women's History Week. In 1987, we led the successful campaign to have the entire month of March declared National Women's History Month.

The NWHP ultimately produced a catalogue of women's history supplies so that teachers of all school levels—from kindergarten to college—could select materials and formulate age-appropriate lesson plans. Posters, pencils, cards, and sweatshirts declaring *Write*

---

[113] Ibid., p. 87; "Misusing History,"
Washington Post editorial, June 9, 1986.

Women Back Into History were shipped in quantity from Santa Rosa, California, and in recognition of MacGregor's work on school curricula, the U.S. Department of Education gave NWHP seven grants between 1981 and 1986—over half a million dollars' worth. The impact of visionaries such as MacGregor may be seen in other initiatives today: For example, Crayola ® offers free, downloadable coloring-book pages of famous women for Women's History Month. During March 2011, a child (or a professor like me) could enjoy coloring in the stern but ebullient faces of Joan of Arc, Susan B. Anthony, Dr. Elizabeth Blackwell, Sojourner Truth, and others.

The Fairness Industry

For all the production of accessible, classroom-ready work on women, change proved incredibly slow throughout the 1980s and 90s—too slow for husband and wife team David and Myra Sadker, tireless advocates for sex equity. In 1994, their book *Failing at Fairness: How America's Schools Cheat Girls* pointed to the continuing absence of women's history in standard school textbooks. By then over 20 years had passed since Title IX became law, assuring the nation's students that no school receiving federal funding could discriminate on the basis of sex. But did that law mean that women and girls would have equal representation within the pages of schoolbooks? Even as women's history graduate programs and conferences were flourishing, little seemed to be trickling down to middle schools. In their research, the Sadkers found that images of women remained inaccurate or even demeaning when they appeared at all.

> During the summer of 1992 we analyzed the content of fifteen math, language-arts, and history textbooks used in Mary-

land, Virginia, and the District of Columbia.... A 1989 upper-elementary history textbook had four times as many males pictured as females. In the 1992 D.C. Heath Exploring Our World, Past and Present, a text for sixth graders, only eleven female names were mentioned, and not a single American adult woman was included. In the entire 631 pages covering the history of the world, only seven pages related to women, either as famous individuals or as a general group. Two of the seven pages were about Samantha Smith, the fifth-grade Maine student who traveled to the Soviet Union on a peace mission ... we wondered why Susan B. Anthony didn't rate a single line.[114]

How it breaks down for school books:

Women's History - five (5) pages.
Samantha Smith's Peace Mission - two (2) pages.
The rest of earth's history - six hundred and twenty four (624) pages.

The Sadkers' work was followed by a series of other studies, including a report from the AAUW (American Association of University Women), critical of how schools prepared girls. Some parents and educators called for a return to sex-segregated learning, believing girls (and some boys) would thrive in a climate without the competitive distraction of the opposite sex. However, the issue of learning styles ignored the larger question of whether women's history as a subject was taught, or tested, in any school. And a decade of focus on whether *girls* were being disadvantaged was rolled neatly into a new focus on

[114] Myra and David Sadker, *Failing at Fairness: How America's Schools Cheat Girls*. New York: Charles Scribners' Sons, 1994; p. 72.

ways *boys* were failing, particularly inner-city youth. It remained far too easy for women's history to be seen as a luxury in overburdened schools, especially in the U.S. climate of No Child Left Behind, introduced by the administration of President George W. Bush.

Where Can You Get a Graduate Degree in Women's History?

Despite the backlash against women's studies and women's history which characterized the 1990s, Ph.D. programs grew apace for the lucky cohort of young women (and some men) who decided to pursue graduate work on women's lives. The growth of the internet meant not only accessible databases and online materials, but discussion groups, memberships, and networking beyond everyone's wildest dreams. Early in the internet era (1996: a year when many state universities still lacked email services for faculty), I found online discussions about the best graduate programs in women's history, with friendly rivalry between scholars, each eager to praise her own institution: Check out the University of Iowa! No, no, come to Michigan State University! How about the University of North Carolina at Chapel Hill? A staggering list of course offerings, women's history student-support groups, archives, and faculty now tempted bright minds from every state to consider graduate work. Today, according to *U.S. News & World Report* rankings for 2011, here are the top twelve women's history graduate programs in the United States:

Rutgers, State University of New Jersey

University of Wisconsin at Madison

Yale University

University of Michigan at Ann Arbor

University of North Carolina at Chapel Hill

Harvard University

University of California at Berkeley

University of California at Los Angeles

Princeton University

Duke University

University of California at Santa Barbara

University of Minnesota–Twin Cities

What goes on in a women's history degree program? Typically, students take two to three years of coursework in small seminars, each course requiring a substantial paper; then come comprehensive exams (written or oral), leading first to a Master's degree and then entry to Ph.D. candidacy—with a dissertation to write. Let's look at number-one-ranked Rutgers. According to the Department of History website:

> The program in Women's and Gender History at Rutgers helped to pioneer the analysis of gender relations—including the study of men and masculinities as well as women and femininities—and now also includes the study of sexualities. At its inception, the program traditionally focused on Western Europe, England, and the United States. We have expanded the program's global reach by building strengths in Central and Eastern Europe, South Asia, Latin America, Africa, and the Caribbean.
>
> The major provides in-depth training in women's and gender history across national contexts and chronologies, including a range of courses from introductory readings to colloquia in feminist theory and advanced research seminars. Course requirements for the major include: Problems and Directed Readings in Women's and Gender History, one topical colloquium, one course on feminist theory (which can either be a history course or an acceptable graduate course from another Rutgers department, such as Women's and Gender Studies, English, or Political Science), and a two-semester research seminar in Women's and Gender History.

Fall 2010 graduate courses included Seminar in the History of Women ("The aim of this yearlong seminar is to produce a research paper of professional quality,") and the catalog went on to include a formidable 55-page reading list for the major exam, at which a dissertation director might present questions from three categories—for instance, Gender and Sexuality, Private and Public Labor, Families and Households, Varieties of Feminism.

Some of the hallmarks of this one graduate program reflect changes that happened gradually in the women's history field: For instance, including the history of men/masculinities, more of a general focus on *gender* as a category of investigation, and shifting away from a Western model to global women's history. Although most of the original pathbreakers in women's history are still teaching, their own students and the students of those students now constitute three generations of women's history scholars in the U.S. alone. This has meant new attention to "the history of women's history" in academia. How will we make sense of this movement later on? Where should aging professors archive their personal papers: Together? By institution? As we change the language we use to understand women's lives, how does that affect research? For instance, the Library of Congress is now set up to identify the *first wave, second wave,* and *third wave* of American feminism. But do all women's histories worldwide fit into those datelines? What of the women whose "waves" were brought on by the Islamic Revolution in Iran; or the beginning and end of apartheid policy in South Africa; or the division of Korea into North and South; or treaties which led to the loss of Native sovereignties?

As new "waves" of graduate students train to teach women's history, the tough academic job market means that only a few Ph.D. candidates will end up as tenured professors. But if the goal is to have women's history courses (and majors) permanently available in colleges worldwide, there will be ongoing need for dedicated, outstanding faculty prepared to teach this material. Those who teach women's history at any level—middle school, high school, college—know the transformative power of introducing students to their foremothers' history for the first time. And for a peek into such moving encounters, we turn to the next and last chapter.

Chapter Five

What's the Impact of the Field? Responses From Students and Scholars

How far have we come? There's still a long way to go. Equal opportunities for women abound—yet equal representation lags far behind. In the United States, over 51 percent of the population is female, and since 1980 more women than men have voted in every presidential election. But in 2011, women made up just 13 percent of the Senate and less than 17 percent of the House of Representatives. It's taken 30 years for a grand total of four different women—none African-American—to serve as justices on the Supreme Court. (I was halfway to earning a women's studies degree before the first female justice, Sandra Day O'Connor, was appointed in 1981.)

Having equal opportunity to pursue a career is also no guarantee of learning about those first female role models who forged a way for other girls and women to follow. For example, today's young American women compete at the top level of athletics, and also serve in the military, where many do see active duty in combat situations. However, a girl growing up in the United States is not necessarily exposed to images or information about female athletes and soldiers in America's past—whereas images of heroic *men* in these roles abound, and are thoroughly incorporated into public museums, monuments, ads and popular culture. This means that *boys* who aspire to be athletes, soldiers, or politicians will grow up learning about men in these fields: Males may draw on the accomplishments of those who went before them. Girls are far less likely to learn about their own historical role models. This phenomenon, discussed at length in the work of historian Gerda Lerner, suggests that one of the tools of women's oppression is denying them knowledge of their past.

Just try to find a statue of a woman here in the nation's capital.

One course I teach at George Washington University is called Women and War, and the first assignment requires students to visit the Women's War Memorial Museum at nearby Arlington cemetery. My goal to raise students' awareness of how seldom we see images of female heroes in public places. Even those who are already women's studies majors (or who have enlisted in the military) are flabbergasted to discover this museum, ten minutes from their campus, dedicated to women's contributions in every war since the American Revolution. Why hadn't they known? And why was the museum such a hidden feature within otherwise well-trafficked Arlington cemetery? They are astounded to learn that the *women's* war memorial is entirely funded by private donations, while the surrounding monuments to male heroes are government-supported. It's really up to women to remember women; yet that puts the burden of subsidizing our public history on the wallets of the underpaid sex.

When my spring 2011 class toured the local memorial to female soldiers, they were eager to share their concerns and criticism:

Kristi

After walking through the Women in Military Service Memorial Exhibit at Arlington National Cemetery, I realized that some elements created an almost sugar-coated portrayal of women's experiences. It presented material in a manner similar to what women must do on a daily basis—the exhibit worked to keep hardship and suffering private, while also maintaining a presentable, pleasant demeanor on the surface.

Sarah D.

I had a difficult time reading the small-print captions—probably a space-saving technique, but I couldn't help but wonder if the small print and lack of details symbolized something larger. I began to ponder the connections between the tiny font in the exhibits and the general public's minimal awareness of women's contributions to war efforts throughout history.

Elizabeth

In comparison to an exhibit on the Founding Fathers or men in earlier wars, it seemed that the lasting impacts of individuals' accomplishments were being ignored. This brings into question the ambiguity over how to display women's history to the general public. It left me wishing their names were at least in bigger print.

.

Tory

Why had it taken me so long to become aware of my sisters at war? At the risk of sounding cliché, they were some brave broads. The world needs more museums so that women can emerge from the "textbook footnote" syndrome.

Olivia

I would like a short blurb on why it took so long to build a women's memorial. I was told by the woman who worked there that one reason the memorial began was women who served in World War II realized they were all dying off without ever being recognized. If they hadn't done something about it, nobody would have.

Sarah R.

I gave myself two hours to walk through this memorial, and it took me twenty minutes. It looked like a seventh-grade class constructed this memorial together as a project for Women's History Month.

Zoe

I resent establishments such as this for dividing women's and men's history so much that I feel unequal, as if women were an afterthought. However, by the end of the exhibit, the curators had

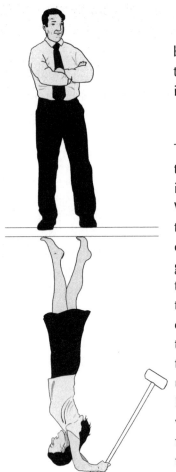

brought so much attention and honor to women's issues in the military that inevitably I felt proud to be a woman.

Samantha

The woman who guided me served in the Marines for 22 years before working at the memorial, and told me the Women's Memorial was established in that particular building in 1997 because it was abandoned. This lack of government support for women's history is shown by the cramped cases that document important historical events, unelaborated upon. If you go to Arlington in the spring, the walkway through the gates actually takes you up and over the Women's Memorial. Look below you and you see the women who served, risking their lives for our country. They're trapped under the glass ceiling, but you are walking freely above.

The struggle to put women's history into public venues isn't just about financial clout. For 75 years an elegant bust of America's most prominent suffragists—Elizabeth Cady Stanton, Lucretia Mott and Susan B. Anthony—languished in the basement of the U.S. Capitol building, forgotten. Carved into seven tons of marble and known as the Portrait Monument, it was formally dedicated in the Capitol Rotunda in 1921, then removed to storage in the crypt the very next day. Louise Schiavone of CNN explains the story this way: "The statue, dubbed by critics 'Three Ladies in a Bathtub,' first stood in the rotunda in 1921. But it was removed shortly after by an all-male Congress."[115] An entire action committee had to be

---

[115] "Even in Stone, Suffragettes Cause a Stir on Capitol Hill." CNN.com, May 10, 1997.

formed to move these ladies from dust to daylight. It took a special act of Congress, with the additional proviso that the statue could only remain upstairs for one year, and on Mothers' Day 1997, the seven-and-a-half-ton suffrage statue finally moved up to the rotunda—with a rededication ceremony following in June. Joan Wages, involved in both the statue campaign and the push to build a National Women's History Museum, recalls: "One congresswoman said she objected to the suffrage statue because the

The monument you never knew you had?

women were ugly. To which Congresswoman Patricia Schroeder replied, 'Has anyone looked at Abe Lincoln?'"[116]

At that time, only five of 197 statues in the U.S. Capitol building featured women. The victory of the suffrage statue was not without dissent amongst feminist activists; the National Political Congress of Black Women, led by C. Delores Tucker and Representative Alcee Hastings, argued for the additional representation of Sojourner Truth and introduced bill HR52 to commission her statue.

In March and April 2011, another series of investigative articles in *The* Washington *Post* informed readers that: "Of the 5,193 public outdoor sculptures in the United States, only 394, or less than 8 percent, are of women."[117] The effort to add a sculpture of abolitionist Harriet Tubman to the National Statuary Hall in the U.S. Capitol had just failed—despite the absence of a single African-American statue out of the one hundred in the Capitol. The Maryland Historical Society refused to replace a statue of former slave owner John Hanson with one of Tubman, who was born into slav-

---

[116] For information on helping to build the National Women's History Museum, go to www.nwhm.org.

[117] Cari Shane, *Washington Post,* April 17, 2011; p. E1.

ery in Maryland. The *Post*'s story included interviews with Lynette Long, founder of EVE (Equal Visibility Everywhere); Notre Dame University professor Erika Doss, author of *Memorial Mania;* University of Pittsburgh art historian Kirk Savage, author of *Monument Wars;* and former Army first lieutenant Diane Evans, a head nurse in Vietnam who led the nine-year campaign to build the Vietnam Women's Memorial. Evans recalled, "We were told by J. Carter Brown, the head of the National Gallery of Art in Washington, D.C., that a women's statue would upset the delicate balance of tension at the Vietnam Memorial." In such ways, women are written out of history.

"We were here too!"

This question of *public representation* is not a trivial one. As long as schools fail to introduce all students to women's history in the K–12 classroom, as long as college courses in women's history are only available to the privileged members of the global population who attend college (and the tiny number of students, worldwide, who go on to do advanced graduate work in women's history), then *public images* of women in history matter all the more. Statues, monuments, museums, public-television programs, posters, even stamps commemorating famous women convey instant meaning to the onlooker: *We were here. We, too, made his-*

tory. Lynette Long adds, "Girls can't be what they can't see." Today, the few statues of women in Statuary Hall at the U.S. Capitol include nonthreatening figures such as missionary Mother Joseph, Sacajawea (added in 2003), and a young Helen Keller (added in 2009).

But images of politically important women remain controversial in our society, for reasons that go all the way back to Biblical ideals, as discussed in Chapter One. As I write during May 2011, Hillary Clinton's image has been erased from a news photo in an ultra-Orthodox Jewish newspaper, *Der Tzitung,* which later apologized to the White House and the State Department: "In accordance with our religious beliefs, we do not publish photos of women.... Because of laws of modesty, we are not allowed to publish pictures of women...."

On the policy of not showing pictures of women.

For those students who are indeed fortunate enough to make it into college and then into their very first women's history class, such academic exposure is life-changing. During the many years I've taught Women in Western Civilization at George Washington University, each fall enrolling 120 first-year college students, I've watched young women (and men) awaken to a heritage they never knew about. Some students react with anger: Why hadn't they known? Who kept this information from them until now, and why? Others are radiant with pleasure and an ineffable sense of homecoming. And quite a few race to my office hours to share what this topic means to them. Here are some of their stories:

Cierra

Throughout my younger school years, no teacher ever sat us down and said, *This is women's history.* But of course, we learned about women role models and women who helped people throughout history. However, these women were considered part of world or American history, never in a category of their own.

The most remarkable women I learned about were Rosa Parks, Maya Angelou, Abigail Adams, Susan B. Anthony, Eleanor Roosevelt, Sojourner Truth, and Harriet Tubman. I always assumed that because I grew up in a poor African-American neighborhood, the schools thought we would relate best to African-American leaders, slavery, and the civil rights movement. It wasn't until I took Art History in 12th grade that I learned about one of my favorite female figures, Margaret Bourke-White. Her photographs are amazing, and she was the first female photographer to be hired by *Life* magazine. After learning about her, my passion for other amazing women grew, and then I learned about the Women's Studies program at GWU and knew I had to go there and learn more.

I never knew Women's Studies was an actual real thing you could have a degree in until I got to college. So, really, I was surprised by all of it; I was surprised by how far back women's history could be dated—that detailed accounts of women had been documented, and that there were actual textbooks written exclusively about women's history! I also found myself disappointed that I had to wait so long to find this out. I was one of the lucky ones to make it out, but many other young girls like me did not, and will never know all this wonderful information about how women have been fighting for years to give us the rights we have today—or why all women around the world are treated and viewed as they are. Hatshepsut, Christine de Pizan, Hildegard of Bingen, Mary Wollstonecraft, Emily

Dickinson, and Alice Paul are all women everyone should learn about in high school. How can we expect young girls to want to be leaders when you don't teach them about these women, who proved they could do anything they set their mind to?

The topics that excited me most were the women of ancient civilization like Egypt, Greece, and Rome. It was interesting to see how the laws and cultures of these civilizations influenced the next centuries. I also loved how some of these civilizations gave women freedom, compared to other cultures. This has inspired me to study abroad in Greece.

Women's history fueled the passion in my heart and led me in what I feel to be the right direction.

Elizabeth H.

After taking a course on Women in Africa my freshman year, I feel my understanding of women in society (and what kind of history is important) changed drastically. After being able to wrap my mind around gender as a socially constructed norm in precolonial African societies (with their female husbands and male daughters), I was able to transcend some boundaries of Western thought to identify women's agency in seemingly restrictive circumstances. I gained important insight into how different women saw personal needs and success, and then how they were able to walk lines of cultural exchanges through personal relationships. This, to me, was a more human understanding of history: beyond the laws and generalizations to what life was actually like for these women, and how they utilized great ingenuity and agency.

Diana

There was one issue that really struck me during this class on women in Western civilization. I was introduced to the fact that women differentiated themselves from other women in order to lift themselves up in society. Elite women were encouraged to distinguish themselves from the poor, white women from black, and modest women from prostitutes. Women spent so much of their time not only warring against male-dominated society for rights, respect and independence, but they also warred against other women.

Women have always represented roughly half the population. On sheer numbers alone they could have had significant power if they were able to band together and work as a united group. I will remember to work as a united group and not as an individual faction.

Andrew

What I will take from the class is a more conscious, top-of-mind view of a society less gender-equal than I believed before. For instance, this morning I was at the Supreme Court listening to a case I'm interested in. It really struck me as I looked up at the black-robed justices behind the large, omnipotent bench that I was staring at a bunch of old men. It literally took me a minute to notice Justice Ginsberg, a petite, frail-looking woman. [Andrew shared this in 2006, after Justice Sandra O'Connor had left but before Justices Sonia Sotomayor and Elena Kagan were appointed.]

Lauren

I learned how the worship of a woman's body has changed drastically from Neolithic times. The modern world relies on women being small, but our ancestors worshipped women who were more robust. I now look at my own life in a significantly different way—I need to ignore media pressures to be stick-thin!

Eleanor

Growing up in the Texas public-school system, my education mainly consisted of the history of men. Interspersed among these influential and historical males, I often learned about their accomplished wives, such as Abigail Adams or Lady Bird Johnson. The women who had the good fortune of actually being discussed for more than two minutes in a class held the traditional role of wife, nurse, or mother. In comparison, my classes would dedicate whole weeks to past presidents. I was left angry and frustrated, wondering why half of human history has been omitted from our textbooks, glazed over or completely ignored by administrators and teachers. Why was I never taught for whole weeks about women such as Hildegard of Bingen or Margery Kempe?

Gina

This was my first women's history class. What surprised me the most was the lecture on the rise of Christianity. I do not consider myself to be a religious person. So it surprised me to think of how Christianity could have *helped* women, and put a new light on a topic I have always looked at with skepticism. I'd looked at the Church as being corrupt, but that lecture gave me clarity as to why Catholicism drew in women at a time when death during childbirth was common—becoming a [celibate] nun was an escape from societal norms, which viewed women solely as necessary to the reproductive process.

Cameron

My favorite part was when we studied the suffragettes. I do think that studying these women—who believed so strongly in something that they were willing to go to jail, go on hunger strikes, and then be force-fed—will stay with me forever. I can only hope that one day I will be so committed to a cause that I, too, will endure hardship to achieve something really worth fighting for.

Amy

Alice Paul made the biggest impression on me. I am in awe of her perseverance and strength: She is a true American hero, and I left our discussion of the film *Iron Jawed Angels* feeling empowered as well as disgusted by the past treatment of women. Our viewing of that film could not have had better timing. I watched it right before casting my vote in the election—with a greater sense of gratitude.

Morgen

What interested me was the life if the *average woman*. In history you often only study the kings and queens, or the wealthy in society. I had never asked myself what a typical person did every day—or about the beliefs men in the earliest civilizations had about women as creators of life. This class really opened my eyes to different ways of studying history.

Ashley

The most important thing I learned was the significance of having an opinion. For too long I was fairly convinced that what I thought didn't matter, wouldn't have an impact, and couldn't affect others. But my eyes have been opened to crucial women in history who influenced many people by standing up for their opinions and fighting for the right to have them.

Lindsay

Because my mother was a women's studies minor, I heard all about the trials and tribulations that women went through in history to have the rights we enjoy today. But there is a difference to learning it firsthand. In the first half of the semester, when we were learning about women in the medieval world, I would always leave class feeling sad or upset. However, once we started studying women's triumphs and the feminist movements, I felt a sense of hope come over me. We have come so far.

Ariel

What I am going to take away from this class is a newfound pride in being a woman. This class was certainly the first time I have learned about history from a female perspective, and because of it I feel a greater sense of identity. Each and every time I go to class, participate in internships and jobs, and especially vote, I know that I will really recognize what it took to get me there. I am lucky to have had so many women paving the way for me.

Occasionally, something happens in class that seems to link successive generations of women in a particularly special way.

Such was the case in fall 2008.

After many, many years of using the women's history textbooks written by Gerda Lerner, I found Lerner's own granddaughter, Sophia Lapidus, in my Women in Western Civilization class at GWU. I asked Sophia to open the book we use in this survey course—Lerner's *The Creation of Feminist Consciousness*—and there was the dedication, which reads, "To my grandchildren, to whom the impossible will seem commonplace: SOPHIA and JOSHUA, REED and CLAY." Incredibly, Sophia had not been aware that her famous grandmother dedicated a book *to her*.

We began studying it together. I was keenly aware of the responsibility entrusted to me, interpreting another historian's work for the benefit of her own granddaughter. But what was most exciting was that as Sophia progressed through that challenging semester, she saw her grandmother in a new light—and approached me about the possibility of interviewing her. Dozens of women's history journalists had profiled Gerda Lerner through the years—but now, fresh interest was being expressed by someone truly close to her. And so, at 88 years of age, having spent her own 18th birthday in an Austrian jail as a young Jewish girl in the anti-Nazi resistance movement, Dr. Lerner sat down to explain to teenage Sophia how she came to write books about the history of women.

SOPHIA: How did you identify and organize material about female learning through the ages?

DR. LERNER: When I write a book, I write it because there are questions I want to ask, and I want to find out the answer.... In this case I wanted to know why it took so long for women to realize they were oppressed and to fight against this oppression.

If you look at the books I wrote before, I studied the lives of American women and watched how they went through a stage-by-stage process of each individual woman discovering that something is wrong. After they got to where they realized they were not alone, they begin to arrive at a feminist consciousness. What was wrong is not a personal problem alone; it is a problem of all women. The idea of power women cannot even begin to think of until a later stage. At the beginning, they do not start out with power; they want an opportunity.

When women finally began to write down their ideas, they were usually not published or available for other women to read and get support.... Women remained, until the nineteenth century, largely ignorant of the contribution and ideas of other women. Each woman had to start all over again from what Christine de Pizan had done, because they didn't know Christine had done it.

SOPHIA: You convey how isolated women were for most of the centuries of history. This is what I have understood: first, male oriented institutions deprived the majority of women the opportunity to learn, ensuring their own power. Then—your definition of feminist consciousness—women recognize that their subordination is not natural, but imposed on them. And you also add how women develop their own concept of how to live as empowered people.

DR. LERNER: Yes. My definition of feminist consciousness is based on the sources that I studied—I did not have that definition when I started writing the book. I did not know what I would find. I had no idea that I would find 1,000 years of women's Bible critics. No one told me it existed. However, when I started reading material from every century, I found there was a woman sitting some place and the only book she had access to was the Bible. Each woman, on her own, worked her ways through the ideas about women, Eve, the Fall, and decided this wasn't right. No woman knew that other women were doing the same thing. Yet when they got together, they were excited to see that other women felt the same way.

Sophia's interview with her grandmother, which eventually became a fine term paper for my class, represented the culmination of a great circle. As Lerner herself discovered, in each generation, women must rediscover the work of those who went before them. And that rallying cry, *Why didn't I know?*, frequently becomes the incentive to take action—to make sure others learn.

In Conclusion

Women gave birth to and nurtured human life and human civilizations. Yet their contributions remain missing or masked in museums, textbooks, images. The history of women, who today make up almost 60 percent of college enrollment in the United States, is still a *special topic,* viewed with suspicion in the academic world, just as *special interests* are in government. Women who wish to *specialize* in women's history have to put considerable effort into defending why it's a worthy topic at all. Thus, each new generation still has to discover anew information that would otherwise remain unseen and unspoken—or, as my student Tory put it, a "textbook footnote."

The result of holding back academic perspectives on women's history until a student arrives at college is that our brightest minds start off intellectually underprepared to function in a world with women leaders. Young women arrive in my classes with high SAT scores and long resumes, completely unfamiliar with basic background on women in world heritage. My challenge, each fall, is to convince them that No Women Allowed, like legalized racial segregation, really did happen—even right here in the nation's capital. "No way! That's crazy!: That couldn't possibly be true," is a familiar outburst, followed by the more accusatory: "You're making that up." Am I exaggerating? Inventing? Indoctrinating? No. But encountering the new and unfamiliar can feel threatening to a bright student who, above all, wants to *do well on the exam.*

To cite bell hooks' book title, teaching "from margin to center" means introducing material that shows social reality from the underrepresented group's viewpoint. When I ask students to write papers about *women* in history, I'm asking them to shift the way history is told—not to reach for the easily accessible, top-heavy mainstream history of famous men, but the marginalized herstory of, say, women who fought for the right to learn. Never mind the history we all think we know; what else was going on—over there, on the women's side? And who's invested in having that history untold, or forgotten? What happens at the margins isn't always marginal, not to the people who live there. Something as simple as sitting down at the end of a woman's workday can be a statement powerful enough to launch a civil rights movement, toppling 100 years of law, and custom, oppression, and shame. Just ask Rosa Parks if what one woman does matters.

Go back and try taking that test in the Introduction. You'll pass. Then launch a revolution of your own.

THE FOR BEGINNERS® SERIES

AFRICAN HISTORY FOR BEGINNERS:	ISBN 978-1-934389-18-8
ANARCHISM FOR BEGINNERS:	ISBN 978-1-934389-32-4
ARABS & ISRAEL FOR BEGINNERS:	ISBN 978-1-934389-16-4
ART THEORY FOR BEGINNERS:	ISBN 978-934389-47-8
ASTRONOMY FOR BEGINNERS:	ISBN 978-934389-25-6
AYN RAND FOR BEGINNERS:	ISBN 978-1-934389-37-9
BARACK OBAMA FOR BEGINNERS, AN ESSENTIAL GUIDE:	ISBN 978-1-934389-44-7
BLACK HISTORY FOR BEGINNERS:	ISBN 978-1-934389-19-5
THE BLACK HOLOCAUST FOR BEGINNERS:	ISBN 978-1-934389-03-4
BLACK WOMEN FOR BEGINNERS:	ISBN 978-1-934389-20-1
CHOMSKY FOR BEGINNERS:	ISBN 978-1-934389-17-1
DADA & SURREALISM FOR BEGINNERS:	ISBN 978-1-934389-00-3
DANTE FOR BEGINNERS:	ISBN 978-1-934389-67-6
DECONSTRUCTION FOR BEGINNERS:	ISBN 978-1-934389-26-3
DEMOCRACY FOR BEGINNERS:	ISBN 978-1-934389-36-2
DERRIDA FOR BEGINNERS:	ISBN 978-1-934389-11-9
EASTERN PHILOSOPHY FOR BEGINNERS:	ISBN 978-1-934389-07-2
EXISTENTIALISM FOR BEGINNERS:	ISBN 978-1-934389-21-8
FDR AND THE NEW DEAL FOR BEGINNERS:	ISBN 978-1-934389-50-8
FOUCAULT FOR BEGINNERS:	ISBN 978-1-934389-12-6
GLOBAL WARMING FOR BEGINNERS:	ISBN 978-1-934389-27-0
HEIDEGGER FOR BEGINNERS:	ISBN 978-1-934389-13-3
ISLAM FOR BEGINNERS:	ISBN 978-1-934389-01-0
JUNG FOR BEGINNERS:	ISBN 978-1-934389-76-8
KIERKEGAARD FOR BEGINNERS:	ISBN 978-1-934389-14-0
LACAN FOR BEGINNERS:	ISBN 978-1-934389-39-3
LINGUISTICS FOR BEGINNERS:	ISBN 978-1-934389-28-7
MALCOLM X FOR BEGINNERS:	ISBN 978-1-934389-04-1
NIETZSCHE FOR BEGINNERS:	ISBN 978-1-934389-05-8
THE OLYMPICS FOR BEGINNERS:	ISBN 978-1-934389-33-1
PHILOSOPHY FOR BEGINNERS:	ISBN 978-1-934389-02-7
PLATO FOR BEGINNERS:	ISBN 978-1-934389-08-9
POETRY FOR BEGINNERS:	ISBN 978-1-934389-46-1
POSTMODERNISM FOR BEGINNERS:	ISBN 978-1-934389-09-6
RELATIVITY & QUANTUM PHYSICS FOR BEGINNERS	ISBN 978-1-934389-42-3
SARTRE FOR BEGINNERS:	ISBN 978-1-934389-15-7
SHAKESPEARE FOR BEGINNERS:	ISBN 978-1-934389-29-4
STRUCTURALISM & POSTSTRUCTURALISM FOR BEGINNERS:	ISBN 978-1-934389-10-2
ZEN FOR BEGINNERS:	ISBN 978-1-934389-06-5
ZINN FOR BEGINNERS:	ISBN 978-1-934389-40-9

www.forbeginnersbooks.com